TAIWAN

REPUBLIC OF CHINA

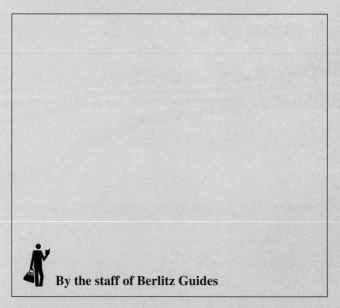

By the staff of Berlitz Guides

HOW TO USE THIS GUIDE

- All the practical information, hints and tips that you will need before and during the trip start on page 97.
- For general background, see the sections The Island Province and its People, page 7, and A Brief History, page 11.
- The sights are described between pages 23 and 80. Our own choice of sights most highly recommended is pinpointed by the Berlitz traveller symbol.
- For hotel recommendations, see the yellow pages in the centre of the guide.
- Sports, shopping, entertainment and festivals are covered from pages 81–90, while information on restaurants and cuisine is to be found between pages 91 and 95, with a special section on reading the menu on page 96.
- The maps are grouped on pages 120–126, with a list of Chinese characters for the main place names on pages 122–123.
- If there's anything you can't find, refer to the index, pages 127–128.

Text and photography: Martin Gostelow
Staff Editor: Christina Jackson
Design: Dominique Michellod
Layout: Doris Haldemann
Additional photos: cover, pp. 20–21, 28–29, 60–61, 75, 80 Taiwan Tourism Bureau; p. 32 PRISMA/ Kugler; p. 44 PRISMA/Schuster/Mayrhofer; p. 89 PRISMA/Westlight 89
Cartography: ⬮ Falk-Verlag, Hamburg.

We would like to thank the following for their help in the preparation of this guide: China Airlines, the Tourism Bureau of the Ministry of Communications, the Government Information Office and the Taiwan Visitors Association. We are also grateful to Gaby Hediger and Paddy Jackson for invaluable assistance.

CONTENTS

THE ISLAND PROVINCE AND ITS PEOPLE

The island of Taiwan lies south-east of mainland China, south of Japan and north of the Philippines. It's neatly bisected by the Tropic of Cancer: the southern tip is on the same latitude as Hawaii. Taiwan is 394 kilometres (245 mi.) long, 144 kilometres (90 mi.) wide, with a shape often likened to a tobacco leaf. Compact in size, the island is packed with contrasts, from the flattest of coastal plains through the living sculpture of terraced tea plantations to alpine peaks capped by winter snows.

More than half the island is taken up by the Central Mountain Range, with its remote valleys and forests of pine and bamboo. Almost all of the 20 million people live in the lowlands, making for one of the highest population densities in

A treat for the children: feeding the carp at Chiang Kai-shek Memorial.

the world. You'll easily believe it in Taipei and the crowded north and around Taichung, where only the signs will tell you where one town ends and another begins. Fortunately Chinese people are gregarious: families like to keep together and do things together. They value and look after their old folk, who in turn can take care of the young. Fathers help as well, happy to share in family duties. And the children are enchanting—the Chinese think so too and maybe spoil them a little.

It's astonishingly easy to get away from the crowd—though people won't quite understand why you should want to. (If you travel alone, you'll probably be asked what's happened to your group.) Leisure in Taiwan has evolved to fit the local pattern of a five-and-a-half-day working week, so facilities—whether beaches, funfairs, museums or hot-spring resorts—are only really

7

busy on Saturday afternoons and Sundays.

Taiwan is cut off from mainland China by more than a sea voyage: after decades in a state of war there's still a political gulf between them, emphasized by the matter of names. The one officially used on the island, the Republic of China (R.O.C.), represents continuity as well as hope. In addition, it affirms by implication that Taiwan is a province of China. On this, at least, old enemies can agree.

Competition nowadays is measured in production and exports, and Taiwan's small population has far out-performed the mainland's 1,000 million or more. A headlong drive for growth has turned the island into one of the "Asian Tigers", around twelfth in the world trade league. Year after year, the economy expanded at an average rate of close to 10 per cent. Diligence, the value put on education, mutual family support, self-discipline, the stimulus of a perceived external threat—all of these have contributed to Taiwan's success. But if there's one magic ingredient, perhaps it's flexibility, as industries move away from crude plastic toys and mass-produced souvenirs to high-

tech and high-value products, such as personal computers.

There has been a price to pay in polluted air and water, ugly industrial and urban sprawl. Not before time, voices are heard urging protection of the many unspoiled regions of coast and mountains and the cleaning up of towns and cities. The reafforestation of the mountains was an early priority which is showing impressive results. National parks have been designated, with more to come, despite entrenched lobbying for unrestricted development.

In this "Treasure Island", as early settlers called it, the greatest jewels of all are its people. It would be hard to imagine where you could find sunnier smiles, or such polite readiness to assist a stranger. When you get lost, as you constantly will if you don't read Chinese, they'll try every way they can think of to help.

Buddhism and Taoism are the predominant religions and their traditions of toleration mean that many temples are devoted to both forms. You can walk into any temple or shrine, and nobody will take any notice as long as you're quiet and don't get in the way. Not that the typical temple is a solemn place: many are like clubs where friends meet and even have a game of cards. The boundary between the sacred and profane is pleasantly vague.

Belief in the supernatural is still strong, despite the veneer of modernity. Deafening fire-crackers by the thousand scare off bad spirits and bring good fortune—to a state-of-the-art computer store. Geomancers are consulted about the alignment of new buildings, where to put the entrance, the offices, even the washrooms. Your hotel floor numbers jump from three to five: four is unlucky—and they may skip 13 too as a conces-sion to Western superstition.

The street scene makes com-pulsive viewing, with its con-stant surprises and juxtaposition of ancient and modern. Next to thunderous traffic, shaven-headed monks measure their length, prostrating themselves again and again in a pilgrimage from one holy place to another, who knows how far away. A repeated, hypnotic musical jin-gle announces the daily advent of the garbage collectors, and just behind a glass and steel office block, a temple fills with the smoke of incense and burn-ing "ghost money".

As well as all this free enter-tainment, and plenty of the paid variety from Chinese opera to "KTV" (you singing on video), in Taipei you can have arguably the greatest gastronomic ad-venture in the world. Every cuisine is here from all the regions of mainland China and far beyond, plus Taiwan's own style, and they can all draw on unsurpassed supplies of sea-foods, vegetables, fruits and spices.

In the cities, it's easy to forget that before the Chinese came, this Pacific island was already inhabited by people the anthropologists call "Austro-nesian" or "proto-Malay" and most others call the aboriginals. Nine distinct tribes remain, liv-ing in the mountains, the south-east and on the little island of Lanyu, numbering in all up to 330,000 (depending on the way you count those who have more or less assimilated). Their arts will remind you of the South Pacific.

Overwhelmingly, though, this is a haven of Chinese culture. There's a strong case for the claim that the island province is in many senses the "real China", distilling the best of tradition and conscious of its role in the continuing history of the world's oldest civilization. At the same time, it has given free rein to the drive and in-genuity of a dynamic people.

A BRIEF HISTORY

Close enough to mainland China to be a natural part of it, but 193 kilometres (120 mi.) or more offshore, in the past Taiwan was often under separate control. And there have been long periods when the authorities on the island regarded themselves as the legitimate government of the whole of China.

Traces of human habitation found on Taiwan date back as far as 50,000 B.C. These people probably originated from the area of southern China, but there was no need for them to make an ocean voyage. During several long periods up until 10,000 years ago, sea levels were low enough to leave a land bridge. Suddenly, about 5,000 years ago, their simple Stone Age culture disappears

Descended from the Polynesians who arrived thousands of years ago, the Ami aboriginal people maintain the costumes and traditions of their ancestors.

from the archaeological record. It seems that those earliest inhabitants died out or were expelled by new arrivals from South-east Asia or Indonesia, probably by way of the Philippines. Part of the mysterious prehistoric migrations that led to the settlement of many Pacific islands, they came in separate waves over a period of some centuries. These were the ancestors of the aboriginal people who still make up a small part of Taiwan's population today.

Ancient records—and Chinese records are about as ancient as they come—show that the rulers of mainland China were already aware of Taiwan's existence, and in the 3rd century an expedition was sent to show the flag. Nothing much came of it, apparently, and for a long time the local population was left alone—though not in peace, for tribal warfare and head-hunting seem to have been common pursuits, particularly among the mountain-dwellers.

11

The First Chinese Settlers

About 1,000 years ago, people who had been forced by persecution from their homes in south China began moving to the offshore islands. Eventually, some of these Hakkas ("strangers") arrived in southern Taiwan and began to farm the fertile lowlands, pushing the aboriginal cultivators inland. During the Ming Dynasty (1368–1644) more settlers came over from Fukien, the nearest mainland province. They called their new home Bao-Dao ("Treasure Island"), but its present name appears at about the same time, at first applied to today's city of Tainan, which is labelled "Taiouan" on early European maps.

As shipping and trade developed in the western Pacific, so did the activities of pirates. Taiwan made an excellent base for their operations: it was beyond the reach of imperial rule and the local people did not interfere. A Japanese attempt to impose order in 1593 proved a failure, but it was a warning of things to come.

European Enclaves

The Portuguese, already with a foothold on the mainland coast at Macao, were the pioneers of European expansion in the region. As early as the 16th century their sailors, passing by on the way to trade with Japan, were impressed by the lovely green island. They called it Ilha Formosa, and Formosa (Portuguese for "beautiful") became the name by which it was known to the Western world until quite recent times.

The Portuguese wanted to set up a fort and trading post in Taiwan but were forestalled by the arrival of their cut-throat competitors, the Dutch, in 1624. Moving north from their new empire in the Dutch East Indies (today's Indonesia), looking for sources of silk and spices and for outlets for their tobacco and opium, they saw Taiwan as a stepping stone to the huge mainland markets. One of the Dutch settlements, Fort Zeelandia, can still be seen, much rebuilt, near Tainan on the south-west coast of the island. As so often in colonial history, heavy-handed missionaries, trying to suppress traditional religion, managed to inflame a basically tolerant people into anti-Dutch revolt which superior firepower contained for a time.

Spain, colonial master of the Philippines, was another rival, putting small forces ashore in northern Taiwan in 1626, but the Dutch soon expelled them. In the meantime, events were in motion on mainland China which would threaten the Dutch presence, just when it looked most secure.

National Hero

By the mid-17th century, the once-glorious Ming Dynasty was at an end, undermined by corruption and battered by invading Manchu armies from the north. But the last Ming emperor named a seafaring southern warlord, Cheng Chi-lung, to command his remaining troops. Cheng's half-Japanese son, Cheng Chengkung, succeeded him in the post and held off the Manchus for many years. He took the name Kuo Hsing-yeh ("Lord of the Imperial Surname") which became Latinized as Koxinga. By 1658, superior Manchu numbers threatened to overwhelm Koxinga but he was able to use his fleet to evacuate a large part of his army to Taiwan.

The incumbent Dutch at first dismissed Koxinga's force as a defeated rabble and no menace to them. So it was a shock when in 1661 he mustered hundreds of war junks and thousands of men and besieged the coastal forts. It took nearly two years, but in the end the Dutch in Fort Zeelandia and the other settlements surrendered and were forced to leave the island.

Koxinga at once set up a government that was a conscious revival of the best Ming traditions. He had brought hundreds of scholars and teachers from the mainland and began far-reaching reforms of education and agriculture. Sadly, he was not to live to see the results, for he died in 1662 when only 39 years old. His son and grandson continued to rule the island until 1683 when the Manchu conquest at last extended its sway to Taiwan.

The Manchu (Ching Dynasty) emperors found it no easier than their predecessors to control the unruly islanders from afar. They might send governors, but could not prevent them from being corrupted, undermined or ignored. Piracy continued, and friction with the West and Japan was aggravated when the crews of ships wrecked on Taiwan's coasts were ill-treated or murdered by the local authorities or by aboriginals. Protests to Peking were ineffectual: officials there could scarcely admit that they had no influence in what was supposed to be part of the empire.

13

Imperial Predators

By the 19th century, it was the British who were exploiting the Chinese appetite for opium. When war broke out between them in 1839, Britain considered seizing Taiwan, but in the end decided to concentrate on obtaining more trading concessions in the mainland ports. The Treaty of Nanking in 1842 ceded Hong Kong island to Britain and opened several ports to British trade. But conflict and confusion continued to reign.

Other powers, notably France, Russia and the United States joined in to get their share of the privileges that were going, and the Treaty of Tientsin (1858) dictated more humiliations for China. However, it included the opening of the Taiwan ports of Keelung, Suao, Kaohsiung and Tainan to foreign ships and merchants. As with the mainland, they were chiefly concerned with selling opium, but in exchange Taiwan was able to export sugar, rice, tea, camphor, timber and coal, and trade flourished.

Far Eastern ports were notoriously free-wheeling in those days, with frequent drunken brawling, but in Taiwan matters were made worse by the lack of firm responsible government. Foreign companies and residents, backed by a variety of Christian missionaries, called for tough measures—meaning intervention by one or more of the imperial powers.

As had happened so often before, in 1871 a ship was wrecked on the coast of Taiwan and most of its crew were murdered by aboriginal tribesmen. But this ship came from the Ryukyu islands which Japan claimed as its own, and in Tokyo there were calls for retribution and compensation. A mission was sent to Peking, but the young emperor (a mere mouthpiece for his mother and advisors) had to admit that the distant island was beyond control. The Japanese sent an expedition in 1874, to try to find and punish those responsible for the sailors' deaths, but withdrew after the Chinese government paid over a generous sum in settlement.

Forced to take an interest in its rich offshore island, Peking declared Taiwan a province in its own right in 1887, but by now influential forces in Japan had acquired a taste for imperial adventure and were looking abroad with covetous eyes. The Japanese invaded Korea in 1894

14

and defeated the fleet China sent to help its northern neighbour. The short war which followed saw the Chinese beaten everywhere: in the ensuing Treaty of Shimonoseki (1895) they were forced to agree to every Japanese demand—including handing over Taiwan and Penghu (the Pescadores) to Japan.

Colony of Japan

The new masters landed a force at Yenliao on the north coast and despite some armed resistance and political protest, soon had the lowlands and towns under control. The rugged, thickly forested mountains proved more difficult—the aboriginal people living there had never bowed to anyone. By 1902 the Japanese decided on a policy of live-and-let-live with the tribes, for the time being.

Elsewhere, discipline and modernization became the order of the day. Like all the imperial powers of the time, Japan persuaded itself of its civilizing mission, and indeed built schools, hospitals, roads, railways, dams and hydro-electric schemes. Some of the best land was turned over to intensive rice and sugar production. As a colony, Taiwan was at first exploited as a mere appendage, a source of food and raw materials and a market for Japanese products. Everyone had to learn Japanese and to take Japanese names. But as the years passed, the colonial masters also invested in the beginnings of industrial development, and this was to give a kick-start to the economy when freedom was eventually regained.

Liberation and Civil War

In Taiwan, the heavy hand of occupation lasted a full 50 years and only the defeat of Japan at the end of World War II brought it to an end. As the Allies had promised long before, the island was at last returned to Chinese rule, on October 25, 1945 (a day still marked by a public holiday, "Restoration Day").

The island's problems were not over. Everyone from official commissions to looters arrived from the mainland to grab what they could of the equipment left behind by the Japanese, from machine tools to light switches.

All was not well on the mainland either. Relieved of their common enemy, the Nationalists under Chiang Kai-shek and the Communists led by Mao Tse-tung now

REVOLUTIONARY LEADERS

The loss of Taiwan in 1895 was only one among many humiliations, results of China's helplessness in the face of foreign demands. Patriots and progressives blamed the weak, corrupt Ching Dynasty court and worked for its overthrow.

Among the most influential was **Dr Sun Yat-sen** (or Sun Chung-shan). Born in 1866, he spent part of his youth in Hawaii, and studied medicine in Hong Kong and Canton. He founded the Revive China society in 1894, but after an attempted uprising in 1895 he spent 16 years in exile, preparing for revolution.

In 1911, the old regime fell, and Sun Yat-sen returned to become president of the provisional government, but unable to unite the country, he resigned after a few months. He reorganized his supporters as the Kuomintang or Nationalist Party, based on the Three Principles of the People: Nationalism, Democracy and Social Well-Being. In 1923 he was able to resume control of the government although much of northern China was in the hands of rebellious warlords.

Chiang Kai-shek was born in 1887 and took part in the 1911 revolution. He met and impressed Sun Yat-sen and joined the Kuomintang, rising to become commander of its army and in 1925 its head, when Sun, the "Father of Modern China", died at the early age of 58.

By 1928 Chiang had broken with the Communists, former partners in revolution, and led a successful expedition against the northern warlords. The 1930s saw intermittent fighting with the Communists and war with Japan, which first invaded Manchuria, then China itself. Chiang's life seemed destined to be one of never-ending struggle but his strict Confucian self-discipline seemed to enable him to keep going in the face of appalling setbacks.

World War II brought the United States as a partner against Japan, and with American aid, Chiang's forces were able first to hold the line, then to drive the invaders back. As one of the victorious allies, Nationalist China in the person of Generalissimo Chiang Kai-shek took part in the conferences that shaped the peace.

resumed their long war against each other.

The two sides raced to occupy the areas vacated by the Japanese and seize their armaments—and in this the

A fitting monument to a towering figure: the Chiang Kai-shek Memorial Hall.

Communists were the more effective. Despite American aid and initially superior numbers, the Kuomintang (KMT) suffered setback after setback. To some extent, the Communists gained popularity with their land reform programme. Although Chiang Kai-shek was recognized as completely honest, the same could not be said for some of his generals and ministers, and at lower levels corruption was rife.

By 1948 the Communist armies controlled Manchuria and north-eastern China. On January 23rd, 1949, Peking surrendered to them. Chiang Kai-shek had temporarily retired from the presidency to allow an attempt to negotiate with the Communists. When it failed, and Nanking and Shanghai also fell, followed by much of central and southern China, he resumed the leadership of the KMT and directed a skilful evacuation of most of his remaining forces to Taiwan. (Garrisons also held out in the Pescadores and on Quemoy [Kinmen] and Matsu, much closer to the mainland. To this day, all these islands remain part of Nationalist China.)

Most of the Nationalists' best troops, their air force and navy, and enormous numbers of their dependants made the crossing. With them came a great entourage of scholars and artists, industrialists and managers, lawyers, doctors and other professionals who were to be so influential in the development of the island province over the years that followed. In all, close to 2 million people left the mainland for Taiwan during this period.

On December 7, 1949, the Nationalist government was established in Taipei, which became the provisional capital of the Republic of China. (Meanwhile, on October 1, 1949 in Peking, Mao Tse-tung had proclaimed the People's Republic of China.) Chiang Kai-shek resolved not to allow the same mistakes that had caused the Nationalists' defeat to be repeated in their new island home.

He began by executing the governor who had presided over the wrecking of Taiwan's economy since the Japanese departure. Education was given a high priority. And those who had forgotten Chiang's revolutionary origins were forcibly reminded of them by a remarkable programme of land reform: many of those who tilled the land became its owners, although the former landlords were well compensated.

In the early years, invasion was an ever-present threat, although the Nationalists bravely asserted that they would sooner or later return to the mainland to continue the fight. The United States had taken a *laissez-faire* attitude to the Civil War and at first seemed to accept that Taiwan would not hold out for long. Then in 1950 the outbreak of the Korean War changed all that. President Truman saw the hand of Peking behind the North Korean invasion of the South and instructed the mighty U.S. 7th Fleet to patrol the seas between Taiwan and the mainland. In 1954 a formal defence treaty was signed between the United States and Taiwan. When Communist artillery resumed the bombardment of Quemoy in 1958, the Americans helped the Nationalists to re-supply the island fortress so they could hit back. (The exchanges eventually developed into a ritual, and in the end the shells that were fired contained only leaflets.)

Economic Miracle, Diplomatic Setback

The government in Taipei took a liberal attitude to trade and industry and Chinese genius for business was given its head.

Behind the shield of the U.S. alliance, entrepreneurs and a hard-working people were able to generate a phenomenal rate of growth. Textiles and clothing, plastics and simple electrical goods came first, but as small companies grew, they modernized and moved into high technology and improved quality. The "Made in Taiwan" label appeared in the markets of the world, and no longer only on cheap and perhaps inferior products.

Industry rapidly overtook farming and fishing in the export tables, but those traditional earners joined in the boom, concentrating on high-value products such as asparagus and farmed seafoods for Japan and the United States.

By the 1960s, American aid had tailed off, and in truth it was no longer needed. The U.S. continued to support Taiwan in the United Nations, where it held the seat allocated to China as one of the five permanent members of the Security Council. But by 1971, President Nixon and his national security advisor, Henry Kissinger, saw advantages in "building bridges" to Peking, and one of the prices to be paid was the withdrawal of its support for Taiwan in the U.N. In October 1971,

Peking's representative was duly seated there, and Taiwan was expelled.

It was a shock and a setback, but the island in the 1970s was very different from the nervous refuge of 1950. There was a new resilience and self-confidence: most people couldn't remember the Civil War and the leaders who had crossed over with Chiang Kai-shek were beginning to retire. In 1975, Chiang himself fell ill; he died on April 5, amid general and genuine sadness.

The old generalissimo was succeeded in due course by his son, Chiang Ching-kuo. Firm and orderly government continued, hand-in-hand with unrestrained commercial expansion. Most of the nations which had diplomatic ties with

Taiwan broke them off as the price of relations with Peking—including, in the bitterest blow of all, the United States itself in 1979. But commercial links were largely unaffected.

New Horizons

In 1987, martial law was finally lifted. Opposition parties began to form and to win seats in elected bodies including the National Assembly. On the death of Chiang Ching-kuo, his former vice-president, Taipei-born Lee Teng-hui, was sworn in as President of the Republic of China on January 13, 1988.

Taiwan is now one of the world's most advanced industrial economies. Its per capita income is among the highest in Asia: its gold reserves are enormous. The trade surplus in the 1980s became so great that missions were sent abroad to try to find products to buy to reduce the imbalance.

Surprisingly, the Communist government on the mainland has welcomed substantial investment from the economic "tiger" offshore. Unofficial and informal but significant links have been forged between the two old enemies, including the declaration by Taiwan in 1991 of the cessation of a state of war with the People's Republic. Reunification remains in principle the policy of both, each of course on its own terms. Who knows what the future may hold?

Pomp and ceremony, noise and colour mark Taiwan's National Day on October 10.

WHERE TO GO

If, like most visitors to Taiwan, you've touched down first in Taipei, you'll want to see the varied sights of the city. But even if your time is short, plan to get out into the countryside, coast and mountains as well. There's a remarkable choice of attractions not far away in the northern tip of the island.

When you decide to go further afield, you'll find that the north–south spine of mountains neatly divides the island into two. It's not only a barrier (very few routes go right across) but a magnet, whose cooler temperatures, hot springs, marvellous scenery and tranquillity draw local city dwellers at weekends, in numbers that can interfere with the peace and quiet. If your tolerance of crowds is less than theirs, try to time your visits to the more famous resorts for weekdays.

Amongst the scale models of great sights at Window on China, visitors seem positively Gulliver-like.

On the east side, the mountains press close to the ocean: in places the sea cliffs are as spectacular as any in the world. Deep valleys cut inland, with scenic roads clinging to their sides. The Taroko Gorge will take your breath away, and so will the altitude if you head for the 3,000-metre (10,000-ft.) peaks.

West of the mountain chain, there's a broad coastal plain of rich agricultural land. This, with it's sheltered waters and harbours, attracted the first settlers from mainland China, and the area is still far more densely populated than the east.

The cities have plenty of historical interest, and they can serve as bases for your explorations, nearby and in the mountains. From Taichung you could visit the old port of Lukang, and then head inland for the resorts of Kukuan and Lishan (from where the Cross-Island Highway can take you to the east coast). Or further south, Sun Moon Lake and Alishan are favourite retreats as well as centres for dozens of hikes and excursions. Tainan has enough historic sites and temples to keep you busy for days. If you're in Kaohsiung, you're probably on business, though an industrial hub of its kind can be worth seeing in its own right. And it's a starting point for the southern mountains, and a stop off on the way to Kenting National Park at the south tip of Taiwan.

For now, we begin with the booming city of Taipei.

TAIPEI

One of Asia's fastest growing cities, with close to 3 million people, Taipei doesn't have a long history. Early settlement in the region was concentrated nearer the sea to the north, at Tamsui (more correctly Tan-shui). The first town within today's city limits was set up in 1875, inside a wall 5 kilometres (3 mi.) long.

The population increased dramatically during Japanese rule and again after 1949, when the Nationalist government moved here and designated Taipei the provisional capital of the Republic of China.

At that time Taipei was an unimpressive place of low and undistinguished buildings. Prosperity and confidence in the 1970s and 80s produced a mushroom growth of highrises and a number of fine public buildings and monuments. The city today is big, bustling and at first confusing, but the street pattern is basically simple. As soon as you can, try taking a walk, even if it's only round the block. If you have a particular objective, ask someone at your hotel or another local contact to write its name in Chinese for you to show when you're asking the way, and always carry a card with the address of the hotel or wherever you are staying.

If your time is really restricted, take a tour to see the highlights. It might be a good idea to take one anyway, just to get your bearings. And on no account miss the unique National Palace Museum (see p. 30).

You'll find several districts contesting the title of city centre, each with its big hotels, department stores, markets and monuments. We've organized the centre into three areas which we've called South-West, North and East, though these are not officially recognized names.

City Centre: South-West

If we choose to begin south of the imposing main railway station, it's because this area was the site of the 19th-century walled city, and it was first to develop in modern times—many government departments are located here. The **East Gate** is one of the few traces left of the old walls, but it's been much restored and is now isolated in the middle of circling traffic.

The lofty **Chiang Kai-shek Memorial Hall** (21 Chungshan South Road) is a stately 76-metre-high (250-ft.) white tower on a triple-decked platform, with a double roof of blue glazed tiles inspired by the Altar of Heaven in Peking. Make your way across the great open space in front and climb the ceremonial staircase. Inside, a seated bronze statue of the late president looks out over the city while soldiers stand guard, their boots and helmets polished to mirrorlike brilliance. The ground level library houses a collection of photographs of Chiang Kai-shek's life, as well as some of his personal possessions. The superbly sculptured gardens and lakes on either side of the square provide a pleasant retreat for mothers to bring small children, who love to throw food to the golden carp. In bright contrast, near the memorial's massive white gateway, the vividly coloured National Theatre and National Concert Hall stand out in ornate palace style.

New Taipei Park is an oasis of shade with a children's playground and statues for them to clamber over. It's notable too for a bust of General Claire Chennault, the American aviator who commanded the famous "Flying Tigers" in the defence of China against the Japanese in the 1930s. He later helped to found Civil Air Transport, forerunner of today's China Airlines. On the north side of the park, the **Taiwan Provincial Museum** (2 Hsiangyang Road) is housed in one of Taipei's few Greek classical buildings. The collections concentrate on natural history—minerals, fossils, shells and stuffed animals—and anthropology, including aboriginal artefacts.

West of New Park, the **Presidential Building**, a curiosity in grey stone and red brick dating from the era of Japanese rule, makes a useful landmark. The plaza in front is used for ceremonial parades. A couple of blocks south, the **National Museum of History** (49 Nanhai Road) houses fine ceramics, and dioramas showing how prehistoric "Peking man" might have lived.

Towards the Tamsui (Tanshui) river in the old Wanhua district, you'll find the **Lungshan Temple** (211 Kuangchou Street), one of Taipei's most important. Nominally Buddhist, it's dedicated to two local favourites among the deities, Kuanyin (Goddess of Mercy) and Matsu (Goddess of the Sea). Although established in the mid-18th century, its venerable appearance is misleading: what you see today was mostly rebuilt after bomb damage in World War II, though some treasures miraculously escaped destruction. The intricately carved stone columns are particularly fine. Lungshan means "Dragon Mountain", and dragons in profusion top every pinnacle of the gracefully curved roofs. To the Chinese, they are not the fierce, threatening creatures of Western mythology. They're friendly symbols of good luck.

Huahsi Street, west of Lungshan Temple, enjoys its notoriety under the label of **Snake Alley.** The street has been roofed over, a blessing on a wet evening. The usual stalls sell toys, clothes and electronic equipment. Eating options range from snack stands through buffets to top-quality seafood restaurants with beautiful display counters where you choose your menu.

You might want to eat first, before joining the throng at one of the snake specialists, in case the operations there should blunt your appetite. Cages filled with writhing reptiles of a dozen species are stacked on the floor, with a mongoose in a basket keeping watch. Part-showmen, part-butchers, the dealers go through their hard-sell routine, pulling out first one snake, then another, lecturing the crowd on their qualities before fixing on a victim and dispatching it with a blow to the head. Small children watch impassively, licking ice creams, and adults who have seen this a hundred times still stare as the snake is hung up and swiftly slit open from end to end. Then the blood and bile are drained into jugs to be mixed with fiery local liquor and served up to waiting clients, who credit the red and green cocktails with the power to cure a range of ailments, sharpen their eyesight and, of course, improve their sexual potency.

City Centre: North

Chungshan North Road is one of the main arteries of this part of the city (note that roads change their names from West to East as they cross it). If you keep in mind how places are related to this road, and to the east-west freeway which roughly follows the Keelung river, you'll be less likely to lose your bearings.

Frequent visitors often choose to stay at one of the hotels in this area, within walking distance of a favourite entertainment zone along and between Chungshan North and Linsen North roads. Fast-food outlets, restaurants and "KTV" bars (see p. 88) are clustered here. So are most of the city's pubs. After dark, some streets and lanes are transformed into a night market focused on food.

The large Taoist **Hsingtien Temple** (261 Minchuan East Road) is decorative and highly coloured. Here, you'll see young secretaries coming in on the way home from work to pray for good fortune, lighting incense sticks and leaving them to smoulder.

The **Confucian Temple** (275 Talung Street) west of Chungshan North Road is much more sedate—the orderly arrangement is typical and intended as an aid to contemplation. In this one, unusually, panels in both Chinese and English describe the life and thought of Confucius and the role of his disciples (the "saints" and "sages"). In contrast, on the opposite corner of the crossroads, the Taoist **Paoan Temple** is often crowded with people bringing in plates of food, which they first wash then leave as offerings on the altar for a while and, with great practicality, take home again.

An airy modern building just south of the Keelung river on Chungshan North Road houses the **Taipei Fine Arts Museum.** As well as travelling exhibitions and a sculpture gallery, the museum is strong on landscape painting in two quite different traditions—one of mountain scenery in idealized form, the other much freer and more colourful.

In a city short on prominent landmarks, the **Grand Hotel** stands out magnificently on its small hilltop north of the

The palatial dimensions of the Grand Hotel make it a Taipei landmark.

river. This rich red latter-day palace with its vast curving Chinese roof was the brainchild of Madame Chiang Kai-shek. Even if you have no other reason, it's worth going up for a closer look, and to admire the view. North of here in the sprawling suburb of **Shihlin**, the day and night markets are Taipei's biggest.

Eastwards along the riverside avenue (Peian Road), **Martyrs' Shrine** honours fallen heroes of China's wars. Built in Ming Dynasty style, it's superbly set against the forested slopes of Yangmingshan. East again and north through a road tunnel, you'll find the **Chinese Culture and Movie Studio**, where fans can visit the sets where their favourite kung fu films and TV historical dramas were made.

National Palace Museum

In the hilly north-eastern Shihlin district, at Waishuanghsi, the finest assembly of Chinese art in the world has found a home, after miraculous escapes amid the tides of war. Its origins go back to the imperial treasures of the Sung Dynasty (960–1279), which have been continually augmented down the centuries.

The museum was set up in the former Ching palace in Peking in 1925. During the war with Japan, the collection was packed into 20,000 steel cases and moved first to Nanking, then to Szechuan for safekeeping. In 1948, many of the most important pieces were among 600,000 items brought to Taiwan.

Just as the museum can only display a tiny fraction of its wonders at any time, you will only be able to take in some of the galleries on a single visit. A good leaflet is available to show you the layout, and you may find it suits you to take a guided tour of some of the highlights (check at the enquiry desk when you arrive). Then you'll be able to return for a longer look, or visit some areas the tour missed out.

The chronological approach is not recommended. It would be easy to spend so long among the ancient **bronzes** and the dauntingly vast galleries of early **ceramics** that you were left with no time for anything else. Instead, as an appetizer, you might go first to Level 3, where many of the greatest examples of craftsmanship and working in miniature are gathered. Look especially for the Ming-period *cloisonné* **enamel** and the later painted enamel— a method unusually learned from the French (the normal pattern being for others to copy Chinese techniques). The evolution of **jade** art is followed from ancient ritual objects to the flights of fancy, often based on Chinese word-play, of the 19th-century masters. See the **snuff bottle** collection, including the extraordinary "inside-painted" glass type, and the incredible carving of *seventeen* concentric ivory balls, each intricately detailed, said to have taken the working lives of three generations of one family to complete. The wonders go on: a headdress where the blue "enamel" is actually made from kingfisher feathers; fruit stones carved into ships—complete with crews. And you are still only on the same floor where you started.

Before you run out of steam, see the duck-egg blue **Sung porcelain** and famous **Ming vases** on the second level, and revel in the brilliant colours of the 18th- and early 19th-century **Chao-p'ing vases.** Back at ground level, a shop sells superb reproductions and books. Modern art is in galleries reached by a separate entrance.

City Centre: East

The broad avenues of the fast-growing, fashionable east of the city are lined with department stores, airline offices and expensive apartment buildings. Chunghsiao East Road is the axis (where the intersecting roads change their names from North to South) and the shiniest developments are along Jenai and Nanking East roads and Tunhua Road.

But don't be fooled by the faceless glass blocks and postmodern towers. Head down a side street (called a "lane" in Taipei addresses) and the atmosphere is more like a village with its own little shops, perhaps a temple or a children's playground. Just like any other part of Taipei, it will sprout food stalls as soon as darkness falls.

The golden-roofed **Sun Yat-sen Memorial Hall** (Jenai Road, Section 4) houses a 6-metre-high (19-ft.) bronze seated figure of "The Father of Modern China", with soldiers forming a guard of honour. An exhibition of historic photographs evokes the China of Sun Yat-sen's time (1866–1925). The auditorium here is the venue for Chinese opera performances and concerts, and

the spacious gardens are a favourite arena for kite-flying.

Expansion to the south-east has almost reached the limit set by the mountains, and here at the edge of the city stands the massive **Taipei World Trade Center**. This futuristic complex comprises the soaring atrium of the Exhibition Hall, the 34-storey International Trade Building, the International Convention Center and a 1,000-room luxury hotel.

Along the Keelung river in north-eastern Taipei, Sungshan Airport no longer handles international flights but is still busy with domestic traffic. This part of the city has its own lively **night market** along Jaoho Street, four blocks north-east of the World Trade Center. Along with the ubiquitous vendors of clothes, toys and snacks, this one features some unusual operators—brush-makers, candy-sculptors, top-spinners—in action. The most coveted stand sites are near the magnificent **Tzuyu Temple**. Dating from 1753, it's east Taipei's counter-balance to the Lungshan Temple in the west.

Taipei's bright lights beckon, even if you can't read the signs.

Near Taipei

The new **Zoo,** one of the largest in Asia, occupies 182 hectares (455 acres) in the south-eastern suburb of Mucha. A shuttle bus will take you to key points—then you'll get the most fun by walking. In the modern way, the zoo adopts a humane policy of allowing some animals to roam in the open. Others are still confined in small cages.

Not many big cities can boast a national park only a short bus ride away. **Yangmingshan**, north of Taipei, is like a miniature version of the great mountain ranges to the south, complete with waterfalls, bamboo forests, hot springs and bubbling volcanic mud. One main road runs through the park from Peitou, up into the hills and then down to the north coast at Chinshan, but if you really want to appreciate Yangmingshan you need to get out and walk. Pick up a good map from the park headquarters, near the entrance to the park on the way from Taipei.

Chihsingshan, 1,120 metres (3,670 ft.), is the highest peak in the park: it makes a challenging morning's walk, but on a fine day the views are worth the effort. (Mornings are suggested because a common weather pattern brings afternoon showers.)

In winter the mountain is often shrouded in mist or soaked by days of rain, but springtime flowers bring the weekend crowds out from Taipei (and on the peak days only buses are allowed on the park's roads). On any fine Sunday, you may be part of a human wave, so choose another day if you're looking for solitude.

In the foothills of Yangmingshan and the northwestern outskirts of Taipei, **Peitou** is a long-established hot-springs resort. It used to be quite separate from the big city, and still feels that way even though it's now officially a suburb. Some of the traditional inns pipe the mineral waters into their bathrooms, others have large communal baths. If you follow your nose to the most active geothermal area—a hell's kitchen of vapours, volcanic mud and steaming waters—you can boil eggs, or buy them, blackened by the sulphurous gases, from food vendors. Uphill from the town centre, there's a **Folk Arts Museum** (32 Yuya Road) with fine examples of most of Taiwan's crafts and a gift shop. You can also tour the **ceramics factory** in Peitou.

NORTHERN TAIWAN

If your trip to Taiwan has to be a short one, be consoled. You can still get something of the flavour of the whole island without leaving the northern tip—even though it's only a twentieth of the area. And if you do have the time to go further afield, the sights of the north will be a wonderful appetizer. Competing tour companies advertise excursions along the north or north-east coast, into the mountains and to several purpose-built attractions, separately or in combination. You can also travel independently: distances are not too great and there are a few more English signs in this region than elsewhere.

South and West of Taipei

It's remarkable how quickly you can get out of the city and into a different world. South of Pitan, set in lovely mountain scenery, **Wulai** is only about an hour's drive from Taipei up a winding valley, and the nearest place where you can see some aboriginal culture, albeit in a highly commercialized form. Wulai's multiple attractions pull in hordes of Sunday visitors, but if you can't choose another day, don't be put off. This is a place where it's just as much fun to be part of the crowd.

Once past the lines of souvenir shops and across the river, it makes most sense to ride one of the miniature trains which rattle their way to the upper village every few minutes. (You can walk, but it's a long haul, all uphill. If you still feel energetic later, walk down.)

The Atayal aboriginals here stage a song and dance show when the visitor traffic makes it worthwhile, and even if the authenticity of some of it is doubtful, it's cheerful and colourful. At the end, they'll invite you to join in the dancing. Most of the village is given over to souvenir and craft shops and dozens of different eating places, all set high up on one side of a deep gorge. On the other, reached by cable-cars criss-crossing high over the valley, are the beautiful Wulai waterfalls. And, on the basis that two attractions are better than one, so is an amusement park called "Dreamland", with fairground rides and a boating lake full of red, orange and golden carp.

Easily reached by freeway, prosperous-looking **Taoyuan** is notable now for the nearby CKS International Airport, and it has plenty of hotels for those who want to stay somewhere closer to the airport than to Taipei. At the airport itself, fans of flying won't want to miss the **Chung Cheng Aviation Museum**. The planes parked outside practically span the history of U.S.-built jet fighters (F-86, F-100 and their successors) as well as other veterans, all in local air force livery. Inside, the story is told through hundreds of fine scale models, replicas and multimedia displays.

Beyond the town of Tahsi lies **Tzuhu** (Lake Benevolence), where the late President Chiang Kai-shek had a country estate. Now his body lies here in a simple polished black stone sarcophagus, waiting for history to change course so that it can go to its intended resting place in Chekiang province on the mainland, where Chiang was born. Visitors in a steady stream walk quietly through the woods to the modest building and make a respectful bow.

The **Shihmen Dam** ("Stone Gate" is the appropriate translation) was finished in 1964, and as the waters rose behind it a beautiful lake was created, less than an hour away from Taipei by road. You can drive most of the way round it, though not very close to the shore. For a closer view, take some of the walking trails, or go for a cruise on one of the boats.

Conscious that children born on Taiwan weren't getting a chance to see the great sights of the mainland that were part of their heritage, someone came up with an answer—build replicas. **Window on China** near Lungtan is the resulting collection, at a scale of 1/25, from the Great Wall to the Temple of Heaven in Peking; even the plants have somehow been convincingly miniaturized. Not content with just the mainland's famous sites, the model builders have added some from Taiwan too. In yet another area, great buildings of the whole world are collected.

Not far away, at the **Leofoo Safari Park**, you can drive or take a tour bus through 75 hectares (185 acres) of well-stocked enclosures. Collect a leaflet at the gate to help you identify the various species. It also tells you the rules: "Don't get off cars or stretch out head and hands" and "Don't feed animals". Despite this, the main objective of the carloads of visitors seems to be to ply the

animals with as much unsuitable food as they can. Children, their faces pressed to the glass, squeal with mixed terror and delight as they push pieces of chocolate through a crack in the window into the paws of a great black bear, or put some cake on the car's roof to attract an ostrich to come and peck it off. It would no doubt horrify animal nutritionists, but it's hilarious entertainment.

The North Coast

North-west out of Taipei along the Tamsui (Tanshui) river, you'll soon come to the port of the same name. Built where the river meets the sea, **Tamsui** (Tanshui) was the site of a brief Spanish presence, at Fort San Domingo, in the early 17th century. The Dutch expelled the Spaniards, but they in their turn were forced out by Koxinga. The fort (its Chinese name means "Fort of the Red-Haired Barbarians") was later used as the British consulate for many years and, although much rebuilt, it still has a distinctly Spanish look.

Taipei residents come here to the fish restaurants, supplied by a busy fishing fleet. The Taiwan Golf and Country Club was the first of its kind on the island. Taiwan's first international champion golfer, known to the world as "Mr Lu", began his career as a caddy here.

From Tamsui, a road follows the coast to **Paishawan** (White Sands Bay). Deserted for most of the year, the gently shelving beach here draws the crowds at summer weekends. After the city heat, they're keen to cool off in the water—and on it in a wide variety of craft from sailboards and jet-skis to rubber rings.

After rounding the cape at Taiwan's most northerly point, Fukueichiao, you'll come to the long stretch of **Chinshan** (Golden Mountain) **Beach**, another favourite for day-trips and camping holidays.

At **Yehliu** (Wild Willows) wind, rain and salt spray have sculpted layers of sandstone into weird shapes. The promontory where they're mostly to be found has long since become a thoroughly commercialized site, and even on a rainy winter day you won't have it to yourself. But you shouldn't miss it: in these popular places the crowd and the facilities that cater to them are half the fun. The entrance is reached through a tunnel of stalls selling souvenirs (spare a glance for the cleverly carved cowrie shells and every sort of dried and salted fish). Out on the rocks, you'll find one area of "mushroom" shapes where softer lower layers have worn away faster and more of the upper layer remains. Probably the single most photographed natural feature in Taiwan, "Nefertiti's Head" does indeed look, from a certain angle, a bit like the famous bust of that ancient Egyptian queen. Rather more odd are the "eggs in nests"—like cups on stone pillars, with round rocks inside. You'll have a good view of the whole area if you climb to the high ground towards the end of the headland. At **Ocean Park**, next to the entrance, sea-lions and dolphins go through their routines of formation aerobatics and jumping through hoops.

Almost adjoining Yehliu, **Green Bay** is the most organized seaside resort on this coast, with hotels, campsites, fairground rides, plenty of sports and plastic bubble architecture. It's nominally a club, and you pay a fee to get in as well as to hire boats, sailboards, fishing or diving equipment.

"Rainy City" is the unpromising local nickname of **Keelung** (which really ought to be written Chilung, the way most people pronounce it). But most of the rain falls in the winter, when the outdoor population goes round permanently swathed in yellow plastic. In summer, there's only an afternoon sprinkle at most.

Keelung is confusing and traffic can get snarled up as it pours off the freeway, heading for the container port. On tours of the north, you'll probably pass through the outskirts, but if you want a view of the port itself, make for Chungcheng Park and the Kuanyin (Goddess of Mercy) statue. Climb up inside the 22.5-metre (74-ft.) white figure for a still better outlook through various little windows. You'll get a different impression entirely in the streets around the harbour, focus of the usual low life of a major port.

North-Eastern Corner

A good day-trip or tour from Taipei can give you a taste of the remarkable north-eastern corner of Taiwan, but there's so much to see and do that you'll want to come back and maybe stay. East of Keelung, **Nanya** is a tiny fishing village, almost hidden in the rocks. Round the next headland, where the rocks rival Yehliu's strange shapes, **Pitouchiao** (just "Pitou" on some maps: "chiao" means cape) is bigger, but when the

Nature has created her own sculpture park on Yehliu's beach.

fleet's in, the sea-stained blue boats are tied up so close together you can scarcely see the water in the beautifully sheltered harbour. Walk up to the temple in the cliff on the south side: as usual in Taiwan's fishing communities, it's dedicated to Matsu, Goddess of the Sea.

Scuba divers rate **Lungtung Reef** as one of the best spots on this coast for colourful fish and coral and brilliant sea anemones, and the offshore rocks shelter a natural swimming pool.

It hardly shows on most maps but **Aoti** (pronounced "Ow-dee") is a sizeable fishing port and town and has some excellent restaurants with tanks of live fish and shellfish, caught or farmed, for you to choose from. Try the "nine-holes"—not a golf course, but baby abalone sautéed in their shells.

When the Japanese forces landed in 1895 to claim the island awarded to them in the unequal treaty of Shimonoseki, they chose the open beach at **Yenliao** to come ashore. A monument to the defenders who died trying to hold them off now stands by the shore. Three kilometres (2 mi.) of white sands from here to **Fulung Beach** are generally agreed to be the best in northern Taiwan.

In summer the sheltered waters of a river mouth fill with the sails of aspiring windsurfers, and the beach, reached by a footbridge, is a forest of sunshades. The little town of Fulung is the headquarters of the North-east Coast Scenic Area Administration, well worth a visit to pick up some excellent maps and leaflets on the trails, plants and geology of the region.

Santiaochiao, eastern extremity of Taiwan, takes its name from the Spanish, Santiago. The coastal scenery reminds Californians of their own Big Sur and the English of north Cornwall. South of the cape, on vast natural platforms of corrugated rock at **Lailai**, anglers line the water's edge in all but the stormiest weather. They say the fishing is uniquely rewarding.

The village of **Tali**, dominated by its huge Taoist temple, marks the southern end of the historic **Tsaoling Trail**. By the early 19th century, land scarcity in western Taiwan encouraged some pioneers to look to the east coast. But there were no roads, only the often perilous sea passage round Cape Santiao. So a path was made, linking Tamsui to Ilan and, although much of it is now hidden under today's highways, the section through the hills north of Tali survives in the original form, paved with stone slabs.

Toucheng is developing as a beach resort: family days by the sea have become more and more popular with the boom in car ownership. The island you can see offshore, **Kueishan,** owes its name of "Turtle Mountain" to its silhouette, a small hump for the head, a large one for the shell. South of here, the coastal plain widens to allow rice paddy cultivation, punctuated by neat vegetable plots and pens full of huge flocks of white ducks being fattened for the table. The busy market town of **Ilan** with a seemingly endless main street is the focus of all this intensive agriculture.

Longer tours continue down the east coast but if you are returning to Taipei, this is where you'll turn inland. **Chiaohsi** is a weekend retreat from the big city where—as in most of the older spas—hot mineral waters have been piped to the bathrooms of many of the hotels. A few minutes away by road, there are more hotels at **Wufengchi**, where waterfalls cascade 60 metres (197 ft.) down a cliff. If you are using the trains, Chiaohsi is on the main east coast line.

The direct road back to Taipei goes through the tea country around Pinglin and past the huge Buddhist Chihnan Temple and monastery.

THE EAST COAST

After you've seen the sights of the north and you want to go further afield, you are faced with a choice: the east or the west side of the central mountains. In this guide, we cover the less populated east first, including the island's top tour destination outside Taipei, the Taroko Gorge. If you're on a tight schedule, you can fly to Hualien, not far from the entrance to the gorge, but that means missing a spectacular journey down the east coast, whether by road or rail. Some organized excursions come to a fair compromise, taking the train from Taipei and returning by air.

South of Ilan, **Suao** benefits from one of the few sheltered anchorages on this coast and now there's a fine modern container terminal and ship repairing facility. But south of the new docks, **Nanfangao** is the liveliest fishing village you could hope to see. The harbour is jammed with trawlers, deep-sea tuna boats and coasters, the quayside is covered with market stalls and the streets are lined with seafood restaurants. The selection is as big as you'll find anywhere in Taiwan, most of it still swimming, jumping or crawling. You'll need a local expert to identify some of the species and, ideally, to help you order.

Suao is the starting point of the breathtaking **East Coast Highway** to Hualien, 111 kilometres (69 mi.) to the south. For much of the way, there's no coastal plain at all: the mountains sweep straight down into the ocean. A narrow track was first carved into the side of the cliffs in the 1920s by the Japanese. It has gradually been enlarged but there's a constant battle to clear rockfalls.

Heading south, the road climbs quickly out of Suao into the foothills and lush, almost tropical vegetation before dropping almost to sea-level at Tungao to cross a river valley. Three times more it follows the same pattern, saving the most thrilling views for the last section, the **Chingshui Cliff.** Here, nature and the engineers have surpassed themselves. The road hangs above the blue Pacific and on a clear day you can see it rounding one headland after another into the far distance, like a scratch on the mountainside.

The **East Coast Railway** from Suao to Hualien, only completed in 1980, is perhaps even more amazing a piece of engineering than the road, and a spectacular ride as it dives in and out of tunnels and over 91 bridges. Although quicker and smoother than the road, its track runs further inland and misses out on some of the best views.

Hualien, the largest city on this coast, has greatly expanded since the improvement in its communications with the rest of the island. The widening of the East Coast Highway, the opening of the East-West Cross-Island Highway and the East Coast Railway and frequent air links to other cities have ended its isolation, and fine new port facilities look like encouraging further development. But it still has a pleasant, spacious feeling and Pacific breezes keep the air fresh. There's plenty to see in and around Hualien, though most tourists only come here on their way to the Taroko Gorge, 15 kilometres (9 mi.) to the north.

Marble quarries near the mouth of the gorge support one

of the area's main industries and you'll soon notice the prolific use of marble, used in everything from the airport buildings to ashtrays. The Buddhist Temple of Eastern Purity on a hilltop near the middle of the city is mainly built of it, and souvenir shops are stuffed with it too. The Taoist **Temple of Motherly Devotion** (*Tzehuitang*) is a rambling, colourful, still-unfinished complex in the western suburbs which brings pilgrims from all over the Far East.

Beaches near the city are stony and the sea is frequently rough. The nearest sandy beaches are at **Shuilien**, 24 kilometres (15 mi.), and **Chichi**, 37 kilometres (24 mi.) south of Hualien. Half an hour's drive out of the city to the southwest, there's boating and fishing on **Liyu** (Carp) **Lake**.

The coastal strip southwards to Taitung is the home territory of the Ami aboriginals, the largest of the tribes with about 120,000 people. Most still live in their villages and cultivate paddy fields, a technique learned from the Chinese, but you'll also meet many working in Hualien. They sometimes put on special song-and-dance performances for tour groups: ask at your hotel.

Taroko Gorge

Just north of Hualien, near the town of Hsincheng, the Liwu (Foggy) river emerges from the mountains, having cut its way for the last 20 kilometres (12 mi.) through a deep gorge that figures among the natural wonders of the world. Taroko means "beautiful" in the Ami language.

The human achievement of cutting a road through such terrain matches the magnificence of the scenery. This section forms the eastern end of the East-West Cross Island Highway, which was completed in 1960 (see p. 55). Since then, work has never ceased, and probably never will, as continual rockfalls from above and landslips below threaten to block or undermine it.

The Taroko National Park headquarters is near the mouth of the gorge on the north bank of the Liwu. It's worth a visit to see their displays on the plants, animals and geology of the area and especially to collect copies of their excellent maps and leaflets.

At the eastern gateway to the gorge, one or two of the local aboriginal women—young with motorbikes and miniskirts, or wizened and even tattooed—

stand around ready to pose for pictures, at a modest fee. On the way through, there are a number of safe stopping places, but if you are driving, watch out—anyone may stop suddenly at any time, including tour buses. Soon after the entrance, look out for the **Eternal Spring Shrine**, honouring the many who died during the construction of the highway. A pavilion built over a waterfall on a steep hillside, it was seriously damaged by the kind of landslide that took some of those lives.

The sheer sides of the gorge seem almost to close overhead at **Fuchi Cliffs** where the roaring turquoise water pours through the narrowest of gaps. Despite the low level of light you'll notice how the bare rockface glistens. The river has carved its complex channel through massive deposits of pure marble.

In the **Tunnel of Nine Turns**, the road-builders sculpted their own way round the face of a soaring, overhanging marble cliff. Here, as at many points along the road, the tunnel frequently becomes a gallery with "windows" into the gorge. Then in one last piece of bravura before the gorge ends, the engineers confidently cut a groove for the road, leaving millions of tons of rock suspended above it with no visible means of support.

Tienhsiang is stunningly set where three deep valleys join. With various hostels, an informal "lodge" hotel and a couple of unassuming restaurants near the bus station, it makes a good base for hiking. It's also where all the excursions to the Taroko Gorge stop—most of them turning to go back to the coast—so daytime can be busy. By evening the crowd has gone and all is peaceful.

A spidery suspension bridge arcs over the river just below Tienhsiang. Cross it and climb the many steps to reach first a white statue of Kuanyin, then a **Buddhist temple** and at the top a photogenic **pagoda** —a perfect example of the Chinese talent for enhancing a mountain landscape with a graceful building.

The road climbs west from Tienhsiang; once out of town look on the left for a prominent tunnel entrance, usually barred to vehicles but open to walkers. It's the start of a short but thrilling expedition. Allow two

The Eternal Spring Shrine is a jewel in the crown of Taroko Gorge.

hours, and take an umbrella or raincoat—whatever the weather—and ideally a torch (flashlight) too, since you have to pass through several long tunnels. Your objective is the **Tunnel of Water**, where a stream flows out of the next tunnel along your route. Water drips from the roof but by hugging the wall, in pitch darkness if nobody has a light, you may just avoid filling your shoes. At the far end, a waterfall pours across the opening. The local name means **Water Curtain** and the effect is beautiful, especially at the rare moments when sunlight filters into the tunnel.

Back on the Cross-Island Highway, a short walk up the road away from Tienhsiang, you'll find a track and steps down to the right leading to a little suspension bridge across the river, just before the third tunnel away from the village. Over the bridge and down more steps to the river's edge, you'll find the **Wenshan Hot Springs**, one of the few accessible sources that haven't been commercialized or diverted into hotel bathrooms. The waters here just feed two pools, one very hot, the other even hotter. There are no "facilities": you change behind a boulder.

South of Hualien

If you continue south on the inland route through rolling green farmlands for 70 kilometres (43 mi.) you'll come to the rural spa of **Juisui,** where the Hsiukuluan river, having made its way north behind the coastal range of hills, at last finds a way through and turns towards the sea. And here, a newer activity has been added to hot-spring bathing—river-rafting. Equipped with helmets and life-jackets, you clamber aboard one of the eight-person tough rubber rafts and head downstream. The river hurries over smooth white stones in a succession of rapids, alternating with lazy stretches of calm water. Several companies run the trips, which take about four hours.

If you vote for seascapes instead, on the coast road south from Hualien more than 160 kilometres (100 mi.) of the seashore and neighbouring land have been designated the **East Coast National Scenic Area**. Quite long stretches are almost deserted but for a few rock-pickers collecting black pebbles. Rocky terraces above the sea give **Shihtiping** (Stone Stairs) its name: they're a favourite spot with anglers.

Pahsien (Eight Immortals) is a complex of caves probably formed by the sea and then lifted high above it when the land rose. Some of them are now occupied by a variety of shrines: with colourful images of Buddha and a Kuanyin statue dispensing spring water, apparently from a never-empty jug. The climb up several flights of stairs to the top of the cliff leads past more shrines at the tip of the headland.

Further south, 112 kilometres (70 mi.) from Hualien, a broad headland called **Sanhsientai** (Terrace of the Three Immortals) faces a strange volcanic islet encrusted with coral. Three of the Eight Immortals are said to have stopped at the terrace and then used the islet as a stepping stone to a legendary home out in the mists of the ocean. Today's visitors can cross by an eight-humped bridge remarkably like some mythical sea-monster.

Just north of Taitung, **Shan-yuan** beach is one of the best on the entire coast, with gently sloping sand. At the southern end of the beach the sand gives way to weird rock formations. Some of them rival Yehliu on the north-east coast—hence the name here of Hsiaoyehliu (Little Yehliu).

Around Taitung

Of Taiwan's cities, **Taitung** is the most remote from the frenetic industrial north and west. People here tend to represent it as a sleepy tropical backwater. The East Coast Railway, improved roads and air links have changed the reality, if not the image, and the completion of the round-island rail link will take the process further.

The wide clean streets are pleasant and uncrowded, but Taitung has rather few claims to make on the tourist's attention. You could climb the hill just west of the city centre to **Dragon and Phoenix Temple** and up the pagoda, if it's open, to get a good view of the area. In front of the temple, notice the massive stone slabs with curved recessing: they're ancient coffin covers, dug up in 1980 during railway construction north-west of Taitung. Further scientific excavation found thousands of artefacts at the site, which are on view at the **Peinan Exhibition**. The neolithic Peinan culture that produced them (and was named after the area) began about 10,000 B.C. and lasted until perhaps 1,500 years ago.

Even those who have had their fill of hot springs ought

not to miss **Chihpen** (sometimes written more phonetically as Jyh Been). South-west of Taitung, the spa is a short drive up a valley from Chihpen town, and its biggest attraction is a complex of large outdoor pools fed by the springs and separated by smooth rocks. One is cool and large enough to swim lengths, the second is hot, and the third very hot indeed. The ideal time is early evening, under the lights hung in the trees around the pools.

And there is more to do around Chihpen—mainly on foot. It's a short walk to the **Chingchueh** (Clear Awakening) **Temple** and monastery, one of the most important Buddhist temples in Taiwan. Two great white plaster elephants stand by the stairs up to a hall, which houses two famous statues of Buddha, one from Thailand made of a tonne of polished brass, the other from Burma made of nearly five tonnes of white jade. The temple also possesses tiny precious relics believed to have come from the ashes of Buddha himself.

A longer uphill walk brings you to the **White Jade Waterfall**, and further along the Chihpen valley rough tracks lead through a forest recreation area where the lush greenery

and exotic butterflies remind you that these are tropical latitudes.

From Taitung, you can head for the west coast by the **Southern Cross-Island Highway**, which starts at Haituan, 60 kilometres (37 mi.) north. It's a fine scenic road, rough in places, taking you across the mountains to Yuching near the city of Tainan. The journey takes all day by bus, in two stages, changing halfway at Tienchih. If you want to break the journey, the China Youth Corps has three hostels along the way, but you need a mountain pass (see p. 111) to stay overnight.

If instead you want to continue to the southern tip of Taiwan, an uncrowded road follows the coast along cliffs and past empty beaches of black sand, through the mainly aboriginal fishing town of **Tawu**. You'll have noticed how the fishermen in these waters favour a strange high-prowed type of raft made of plastic tubing, developed from a traditional bamboo version. Then, until the last stages of the East Coast Highway are completed, you are finally forced to turn inland through the mountains, all the way to the west coast at Fengkang.

Island Excursions

Out in the Pacific, 76 kilometres (48 mi.) south-east of Taitung, **Lanyu** (or Orchid Island) is the home of the smallest of the aboriginal tribes, the Yami. This little outpost is reckoned to be the furthest north that early Polynesian voyagers reached.

Small propellor-driven planes ply regularly, weather permitting, between Taitung airport and the tiny airstrip which has somehow been squeezed onto the mountainous little island. (On arrival, you should reconfirm your return flight and its time, and when you should turn up for it.)

The Yami, about 2,600 of them, live in just six villages dotted round the rocky shore. Sadly, the beautiful traditional thatched houses which you can see preserved in Taiwan's aboriginal culture parks are rare now, but the decorative canoes which have become the island's symbol are still used for fishing. The Yami supplement the catch by growing root vegetables and taro in tiny paddy fields, and raising plump and happy black pigs which root about in the village streets.

Apart from one short cut and a few tracks up the mountainsides, there's only a single road and it follows the coast—after 37 kilometres (23 mi.) you're back where you started. A bus service makes the circular tour: you can get out and walk at any point, picking up the next one about two hours later—bearing in mind that the last service runs in mid-afternoon. Otherwise, you can rent a scooter or negotiate a price for a tour with the driver of one of the island's handful of ramshackle taxis. Take the time for plenty of stops to see the strange coastal scenery of black volcanic rock, intense green vegetation, white surf and blue ocean.

Summers are intensely humid and winters are wet, with a chance that high winds or low cloud may close the airport, so come prepared to stay overnight. Accommodation is limited to two simple hotels (which also have dormitories). If you have the time to wait for it, there's a boat service between Fukang near Taitung, Lanyu and Green Island, nominally sailing twice a week, but again subject to the weather.

Green Island (Lutao), although only 33 kilometres (20 mi.) offshore east of Taitung, seems surprisingly not to have been settled by aboriginal people. Indeed tradition says

that the first inhabitants came from Little Liuchiu island off Taiwan's south-west coast in 1805. Green Island is even smaller than Lanyu—its coast road is only 17 kilometres (11 mi.) long—but more densely populated. Fishing, fish-farming and a little agriculture support about 4,500 people.

Plans are in hand to expand tourism, and certainly the fishing, snorkelling and scuba-diving would be an enticement. There's a simple hotel and hostel at the southern tip of the island near a sandy beach and—even here—a hot and salty spring right by the sea. But most people come only for the day on the small planes from Taitung and take a taxi or bus ride around the coast, making a diversion inland to climb to **Kuanyin Cave**, where a stalagmite somewhat resembles the Goddess of Mercy.

The fishing canoes of the Yami tribe on Lanyu island are decorative as well as functional.

CENTRAL AND WEST TAIWAN

The sea has been retreating on the west side of the island for thousands of years, as rivers deposit their silt and sandbanks build up off the shore and eventually join on to it. Speeded by land reclamation schemes, the process has left once-flourishing ports and fishing towns a long way inland, connected to the sea only by muddy creeks.

Fertile land, flat as a board, is the result all along the west coast. Despite its value for agriculture, industrial and urban pressures have been enormous, and environmentalists have nightmares of all the separate towns joining up in a "megalopolis". But it hasn't happened yet, and city dwellers can quickly get out into green countryside and forested mountain slopes. Increasingly, they have the desire, the means and the wheels to do just that, so some celebrated hot-spring and hill resorts an hour or two away do good business at weekends.

From Taichung, you can take the spectacular East-West Cross Island Highway through the Central Mountain Range to the east coast.

Taichung

Settled in 1721, it was first called Tatun ("Big Mound"): the present name just means "Central Taiwan". With a population of over 700,000 this is the third largest city on the island, after Taipei and Kaohsiung. Its broad avenues have a striking air of prosperity, and with a new harbour only minutes away by specially built freeway, development looks set to continue.

Travelling around Taiwan, perhaps heading south or across the island on the East-West Highway, you're almost sure to pass through Taichung. Try to find time to make a stop, for several sites are worth visiting. The beautiful and tranquil **Martyrs' Shrine** (Lihsing Road), like those in Taipei and other cities, is dedicated to the patriots who were executed during the last days of the old regime before the revolution of 1911. Nearby, the restrained **Confucian Shrine** is a quiet retreat from the frenetic traffic.

In the same area, north-east of the city centre, **Paochueh Temple** (140 Chienhsing Road) is home to Taiwan's biggest "Happy Buddha", 27 metres (88 ft.) tall, and housing offices, a library, classrooms and craft displays. Both the open-air market on Chengkung Road and the night market near Taichung Park and the junction of Kuangfu and Sanmin roads are centrally located.

The **National Museum of Natural Science** (1 Kuanchien Road) stands in a spacious garden setting in the smart north-west of the city. The latest display techniques and "hands-on" exhibits bring science alive, from evolution to the exploration of space. In the Planetarium, remarkable projectors envelop the audience with vast and stunning images. A new **World Trade Center** proclaims Taichung's leading role in high-technology exports. The Taiwan **Museum of Art** (2 Wuchuan West Road) has collections of traditional Chinese landscape and modern paintings as well as special exhibitions.

South-west of Taichung, busy **Changhua** is known for a huge Buddha on a hillside park east of the centre called Pakuashan (Eight Trigram

In the narrow old lanes of Lukang, millions of joss-sticks are dipped in a viscous mixture and laid out to dry.

Mountain). Sitting on a shallow white pedestal shaped like a lotus, the 22-metre-high (72-ft.) black concrete statue is hollow, so you can climb steps inside and look out through the eyes, ears and nostrils.

If you're collecting giant images of Buddha, another of about the same size as Changhua's stands at **Wufeng**, 10 kilometres (6 mi.) south of Taichung. That's on the road to **Tsaotun,** where the Taiwan Provincial Government operates a **Handicraft Exhibition Hall** of traditional products: wood and stone carving, lacquerwork, weaving and embroidery, jewellery and much more. The seat of the provincial government is not far away, in the purpose-built "model village" of Chunghsing.

Lukang was an active port from as early as the 17th century until the Japanese closed it after their 1895 takeover, to suppress trade and immigration from mainland China. Thereafter, it quickly silted up. The effect was to arrest development for decades and leave Lukang looking much as it must have done in the 19th century, although the outskirts are now a tangle of light industry and commerce. It's only a 20-minute drive from Chang-

hua and not much more from Taichung, and a walk round the middle of town today is a delight. You'll see woodworkers producing massive furniture, stone-carvers, calligraphers and jewellers working in open-fronted stores. Look out for brilliantly painted paper lanterns, one of Lukang's specialities. In the narrow lanes, joss sticks are produced by the million, dipped in a viscous brew and laid out to dry. Everywhere, the air is heavy with the smells of incense, camphorwood and lacquer.

Don't miss the **Lukang Folk Arts Museum** (reached from the main street, Chungshan Road, by an alleyway). Costumes and jewellery, silver, historic photographs and documents are beautifully displayed and rooms elegantly furnished the way they might have been in a prosperous family's home in the 19th century.

Many early buildings in Lukang that had survived in daily use for so long were sadly devastated by storms and floods in 1986. Mercifully, the lovely old **Lungshan Temple** (Sanmin Road) with its complex and subtly carved wood ceilings escaped largely intact. Dedicated to Kuanyin, it's one of the earliest in Taiwan. The

Matsu Temple on the other side of the town centre houses an ancient image of Matsu, Goddess of the Sea. It's believed to have been brought here in 1683 or 1684 by the Manchu expedition which extinguished the last flickers of resistance by Ming Dynasty loyalists.

East-West Cross Island Highway

"The Rainbow of Treasure Island", or more prosaically Route 8, heads inland from Taichung through Tungshih. First climbing gently, then twisting and clinging to near-vertical valley walls, it finally emerges from the amazing Taroko Gorge (see p. 43) to reach the east coast.

If you plan to drive right across, allow a full eight-hour day, to give you plenty of time to stop and admire the views. Better still, break the journey by staying overnight along the way.

It took four years and 10,000 men, many of them army veterans who had crossed from the mainland with Chiang Kai-shek, to cut and blast this route through the mountains. The link was forged by 1960, but the battle never ends, as landslides and rockfalls triggered by rainstorms and earth tremors frequently threaten to sever it.

Your first stop might be at **Kukuan** (Valley Pass), a hot-springs resort on both sides of a deep river valley. If you want to take a dip, you'll have to check into one of the many hotels. They've piped the therapeutic waters to their bathrooms, and notices claim them to be effective against everything from arthritis to athlete's foot.

Most visitors to Kukuan head for **Dragon Valley Falls**, reached from the highway by the lowermost suspension bridge over the river. The pretty falls are half an hour's fast walk away, up a side valley, with plenty of steps to climb. (You can avoid some of the steps by taking an overhead monorail train for the first stage, up to a small zoo and aviary.) You'll pass a serene Kuanyin statue high on a rock face, where electronic chanting competes with the music of rushing water, before coming to the falls themselves. Depending on recent rains, the scene is one of roaring torrents and flying spray, or a gentle trickle.

Dragon Valley is quite typical of well-known holiday sites in Taiwan in having plenty of

public conveniences, soft-drink vending machines, signs giving the distances travelled and still to go, and viewing platforms at the actual beauty spot. Back in the village, rows of restaurants specialize in fresh trout: you can pick your own as it swims in a tank, and even borrow a net to catch it yourself.

Beyond Kukuan a succession of dams holds back the river in sinuous blue reservoirs: the biggest, at **Techi** (Tekee), is the site of a major hydro-electric scheme.

Lishan, about halfway along the Cross-Island Highway and at 1,945 metres (6,380 ft.) twice as high as Kukuan, has an almost Himalayan air. The name, meaning "Pear Mountain", is nothing less than the truth. At a distance, the steep slopes above and below the town look as if they are covered in scaffolding. Get closer,

Temples, like the Lungshan Temple at Lukang, aren't only places of worship: they can be playgrounds and child-minding services, as well as senior citizens' clubs.

and you'll see that they're an elaborate network of bamboo poles, supporting dense orchards of fruit trees—pears, of course, but apples, plums and apricots too. In the market square, lines of rainbow-coloured umbrellas cover the stalls of the cheerful traders.

A short excursion south out of Lishan takes you high above the village to **Fushoushan** (Lucky Longevity Mountain) where you can stroll along lanes through fields and more orchards.

Also at Lishan, the Cross-Island Highway divides, and a branch sets off to the north-east through **Wuling Farm,** 1,700 metres (5,578 ft.), actually an area of many farms, orchards and woods and a favourite with hikers and climbers who want to scale **Hsinglungshan**, at 3,884 metres (12,743 ft.) the second highest peak in Taiwan. There are several rustic guesthouses to stay at on the southern section of this road, which then winds down a long valley all the way to Ilan, near the north-east coast (see p. 41).

The main coast-to-coast route, heading east from Lishan, reaches its summit at **Tayuling** (Great Yu Pass) with an altitude of about 2,600 metres (8,350 ft.). If you are going all the way to the eastern end, the most difficult sections and the finest scenery are still to come, believe it or not (see pp. 43–46).

Only 10 kilometres (6 mi.) to the south of Tayuling, a narrow branch of the highway climbs as high as any road on the island, over a 3,275-metre (10,743-ft.) pass on the shoulder of **Hohuanshan**, 3,416 metres (11,207 ft.). January and February snowfalls, when they don't block the road, attract Taiwan's skiers here by the hundred. There's a ski-lift and rough-and-ready hostel accommodation. If you plan to stay overnight, bring plenty of warm clothing: this may be the edge of the tropics but the altitude makes it bitterly cold.

The road continues south, less steep but mainly unsurfaced and torn up by the chains that cars have to use in snow. When it's dry, the traffic stirs up clouds of dust. In the wet or when the snow's melting, it can be a sea of mud. But the scenery is superb, and the route attracts plenty of hikers. **Wushe**, 40 kilometres (25 mi.) from Tayuling, was the site of a 1930 revolt against the Japanese after they reversed their policy of leaving the aboriginal people of the remoter mountain regions to live in their old ways. The uprising was bloodily suppressed.

Wushe sits on a mountain ridge above a tranquil reservoir called Green Lake. Weekenders from Taichung get a fix of fresh air here, or go on a little further to **Lushan**, set in a deep wooded valley where rustic hotels line up along a fast-flowing river.

Sun Moon Lake

You'll soon see why Sun Moon Lake has been a long-established favourite with honeymooners and weekend escapists. At 762 metres (2,500 ft.) above sea-level, it's high enough to make a cool refuge from the humid summer heat of the cities. And it makes a perfect centre for exploration in a scenic area full of happy discoveries.

The lake itself is natural, but enlarged when it was dammed during the Japanese era to produce hydro-electric power. You can rent a rowboat or take a cruise on the clear turquoise water—but not swim. The lake's fanciful name (a direct translation from the Chinese) comes from its shape seen from certain vantage points. Leaving the souvenir shops and hotels of

Sun Moon Lake village, a road to the east hugs the shore. The imposing **Wenwu** (Literature-Warrior) **Temple** is filled with intricate, highly coloured carving and painting, all of it quite new. Two huge stone lions stand guard, their claws on great balls.

Further along the lakeside a statue of Chiang Kai-shek looks out across the water to the nine-tier **Tzuen** (Filial Devotion) **Pagoda**, beautifully sited and built in 1971 on his instructions in memory of his mother.

An aboriginal village near the shore is a modern replacement for one that was covered when the waters rose. Now it's chiefly concerned with selling souvenirs. Don't confuse it with the Formosan Aboriginal Culture Village.

At the south end of the lake, below the Tzuen Pagoda, the modern **Hsuanchuang Temple** houses precious relics of a priest of that name who, in the time of the Tang Dynasty, brought Buddhism to China. The road along the shore ends near here at a jetty, but a walk up to the pagoda gives one of the best views of the lake.

The **Formosan Aboriginal Culture Village** is only ten minutes away by road. At first, you may think you've come to the wrong place, at the sight of a perfect replica of an 18th-century European formal garden and palace. But these, like a laser and fountain show, are just extras.

The "village" itself is a brilliantly realized concept. Nine separate small villages are set on the slopes of a wooded valley, one for each of the mountain or island-dwelling aboriginal tribes whose cultures survive in Taiwan today. Original buildings or careful replicas have been assembled and furnished with artefacts, and then brought to life by the presence of some of their people. It's a matter of luck, what you will actually see going on—some of the villages can be deserted while in others

there'll be weaving, cooking and carving.

Collect a leaflet with a good map of the whole area (the official book is excellent too) and check the times of any special shows. Head to the top of the valley by shuttle bus and just meander downhill, taking in the various villages, from the Paiwan near the top, via the Rukai, Puyuma, Bunun,

Tsou-Thau, Saisiat, Atayal and Ami to the Yami of Lanyu (Orchid Island) by a lake near the entrance.

Mainly at weekends, in the open-air arena above the Paiwan village, musicians and a vividly dressed and athletic young cast give an entertaining performance of dances and rituals, including the famous swinging of eligible girls to terrifying heights on a rope. The music is hypnotic but it sounds as if a lot of Chinese and pop influences have been absorbed. The show doesn't try to be too authentic—especially when the audience gets onto the stage and joins in.

On the way to or from Sun Moon Lake, you'll probably pass through **Puli**, billed as "the geographical centre of Taiwan", but more obviously the focus of a region of intensive agriculture: tea, mushrooms, top-quality vegetables and fruit.

Serene and lovely over temple roofs—it's no wonder Sun Moon Lake is a favourite resort.

More Mountain and Forest Retreats

A favourite with local week-enders and walkers, **Hsitou** (Chitou) **Forest Reserve** is not far east of Route 3 between Taichung and Chiayi. Cool, shady stands of conifers and huge bamboo are the attraction, but there's a drawback—they have grown tall enough to ob-scure the view. Half the hikers photograph the other half on the arc-shaped bamboo bridge over "Great Learning Pond" or looking up a mighty hollow cypress tree, 2,800 years old. Like others scattered about the mountains, it survived the heavy logging of the Japanese occupation and stands surrounded by the results of far-sighted reafforestation programmes.

Beyond Hsitou, **Shanlinhsi** (sometimes written in English on road signs as Sun Link Sea) is being promoted as a recreation area with boating and archery as well as walking.

Your next foray into the mountains might be to **Tsaoling**, a fast-growing resort with a dozen hotels which only come alive at weekends. The village then turns into something of a boomtown of souvenir shops and restaurants. Open-fronted stores sell thin slices of deer antler (for preparing decoctions to enhance male potency), huge

Whether through coloured goggles or the naked eye, watching the sun rise over Alishan's "sea of clouds" is an experience to remember.

sacks of tea and dried exotic mushrooms. Fortified by a mountain diet and the clear air, you'll be in good shape to tackle some of the walks in the area. In places you can ride ropeways like ski-lifts as you head down to the valley floor where waterfalls tumble into the river.

In Taipei, steaming in summer or shrouded in grey winter mist, people dream of **Alishan**. This highest of the popular resorts long ago entered local mythology: to go there almost ranks as a pilgrimage. Most visitors used to arrive by the **narrow-gauge railway**, built by the Japanese so that they could exploit the region's timber. Starting from **Chiayi** at near sea-level, it climbs for three hours, over 77 bridges and through 50 tunnels in the course of its 72-kilometre (45-mi.) journey to Alishan station, at 2,190 metres (7,185 ft.). Rail fans will still want to make the trip, though the schedule has been reduced to one train per day, now that a smooth road has been built and the bus is quicker and cheaper.

When you check into your hotel or hostel in Alishan, they'll ask you if you want an early—very early—wake-up call in the morning and prob-ably offer to sell you a bus or train ticket for **Celebration Peak**, 2,490 metres (8,170 ft.), on Chushan to see the sun rise over Taiwan's famous "Sea of Clouds". A few go on foot and some by minibus but the major-ity will pack into special trains for a half-hour ride to the top. Most days, there won't be much of a crowd, but on Sunday mornings you'll be swept along in an eager sea of humanity. And there's no need to miss breakfast: dozens of vendors will be whipping up waffles, french toast and fried egg sandwiches. Tour leaders with loud-hailers address the throng, taking half an hour to tell them the sun is going to come up, and people even don coloured goggles. At last, a brilliant point of light appears over the eastern peaks and sunlight suf-fuses the morning mists which fill the valleys.

It's an easy stroll downhill to Alishan and if you have picked up a map of the area from your hotel, you can make detours to some of the sights—temples, ponds, suspension bridges and strange trees. The upper station has some of the old 1926 rolling stock on display.

Yushan (Jade Mountain or Mount Morrison), 3,997 metres (13,113 ft.), is Taiwan's tallest

RECOMMENDED HOTELS

Taiwan's hotels are in general well run and give value for money. Service is willing and cheerful and standards of cleanliness and equipment are high.

Hotels are assessed by the Tourism Bureau on a "plum blossom" scale on the basis of comfort and amenities. The top categories include the "International Tourist Hotels", with 5 and 4 plum blossoms; "Tourist Hotels" have 3 and 2 plum blossoms. Many more hotels are not rated at all. Don't take these ratings as an exact guide to quality.

The Taiwan Visitors Association publishes a list of its member hotels, which are mostly in the highest available categories in each location.

Taipei has a vast choice of hotels: you may want to pick one partly on the basis of its location. The city has the reputation of being an expensive place to stay: that is based on the prices of the best rooms and suites at the prestige hotels that cater for international business travellers and the prosperous end of the local market. If you are on a more limited budget, you have plenty of possibilities. We have not listed more than a small fraction of the hotels in our "lower-priced" category, and in practice you could find many of a perfectly acceptable standard at a price less than half the upper limit given.

Apart from Kaohsiung, which has several hotels in each price bracket, other cities offer a very much smaller choice. Each of the better-known mountain and beach resorts has a handful of hotels—and the pattern of Taiwan leisure time means that they may be full on a Saturday night, half-full on a Friday or Sunday, and empty the rest of the week (when you may be able to negotiate a large discount).

The more modest hotels generally don't take credit cards, and you should not be surprised if you are asked to pay for the room in advance.

Prices quoted are for a double room with bath but without breakfast.

||| Higher-priced (above NT$4,000)
|| Medium-priced (NT$2,000–4,000)
| Lower-priced (below NT$2,000)

Taipei

Asiaworld Plaza ▮▮▮
100 Tunhua North Road, Taipei. Tel. (02) 715 0077, fax (02) 71 4148
City centre (north-east). Modernistic towers with huge atrium café plaza.
Pool, fitness centre, shops, many restaurants, conference facilities,
adjoining department store with cinema.

Brother ▮▮
255 Nanking East Road, Section 3, Taipei. Tel. (02) 712 3456,
fax (02) 717 3334
City centre (north-east). Shops, restaurants, conference facilities.

Castles ▮▮
23-1 Hsuangcheng Street, Taipei. Tel. (02) 597 2391, fax (02) 595 1115
City centre (north). Bright modern hotel. Restaurant.

China Taipei ▮▮
14 Kuanchien Road, Taipei. Tel. (02) 331 9521, fax (02) 381 2349
City centre. Shops, three restaurants, conference facilities.

Flowers ▮
19 Hankow Street, Section 1, Taipei. Tel. (02) 312 3811, fax (02) 312 3800
City centre (west), near railway station and shops. Restaurants.

Fortune Dragon/Dai-ichi ▮▮▮
172 Chunghsiao East Road, Section 4, Taipei. Tel. (02) 772 2121,
fax (02) 721 0302
City centre (south-east), near World Trade Centre and department stores.
Restaurants, convention facilities.

Gala ▮▮
186 Sungchiang Road, Taipei. Tel. (02) 541 5511, fax (02) 531 3831
City centre (north). Restaurants.

Golden China ▮▮
306 Sungchiang Road, Taipei. Tel. (02) 521 5151, fax (02) 531 2914
City centre (north). Restaurants, conference facilities.

Golden Star ▮
9 Lane 72, Chungshan North Road, Section 2, Taipei.
Tel. (02) 551 9266, fax (02) 543 1322
City centre (north). Small, modest hotel. Restaurants.

Grand ▬▬ ‖

1 Chungshan North Road, Section 4, Taipei. Tel. (02) 596 5565, fax (02) 594 8243

On a hill at north edge of city. Landmark in palace style with huge traditional roof. Pool, tennis, shops, restaurants, convention facilities.

Grand Hyatt ‖‖‖

2 Sungshou Road, Taipei. Tel. (02) 720 1234, fax (02) 720 1111

City centre (south-east), next to World Trade Centre. Huge futuristic towers, marbled palatial interiors. Pool, fitness centre, squash, shops, many restaurants, entertainment, convention facilities.

Hilton International ▬▬▬ ‖‖‖

36 Chunghsiao West Road, Section 1, Taipei. Tel. (02) 311 5151, fax (02) 331 9944

Centrally located near main railway station and main business district/government offices. Health club, five restaurants, shops, conference facilities.

Howard Plaza ‖‖‖

160 Jenai Road, Section 3, Taipei. Tel. (02) 700 2323, fax (02) 700 0729

City centre (south-east). Large modern block. Fitness centre, tennis, pool. Shops, five restaurants, convention facilities.

Imperial ‖

600 Linshen North Road, Taipei. Tel. (02) 596 3333, fax (02) 592 7506

City centre (north). Health centre, shops, four restaurants. Convention facilities.

Lai Lai Sheraton ‖‖‖

12 Chunghsiao East Road, Section 1, Taipei. Tel. (02) 321 5511, fax (02) 394 4240

City centre (east). Big complex. Fitness centre, pool, squash. Shops and many restaurants, disco. Convention facilities.

Leofoo ‖

168 Changchun Road, Taipei. Tel. (02) 507 3211, fax (02) 508 2070

City centre (east). Four restaurants.

Mandarin ‖‖‖

166 Tunhua North Road, Taipei. Tel. (02) 712 1201, fax (02) 712 2122

City centre (north-east), garden setting. Fitness centre, pool, tennis. Shops, restaurants, disco, convention facilities.

New Asia

139 Chungshan North Road, Section 2, Taipei. Tel. (02) 511 7181, fax (02) 522 4204

City centre (north). Restaurants.

Orient

85 Hankow Street, Section 1, Taipei. Tel. (02) 331 7211, fax (02) 381 3068

City centre. Restaurants.

President

9 Tehuei Street, Taipei. Tel. (02) 595 1251, fax (02) 591 3677

City centre (north). Restaurants, shops, conference facilities.

Regent of Taipei

41 Chungshan North Road, Section 2, Taipei. Tel. (02) 523 8000, fax (02) 523 2828

City centre (north). Modern, large rooms. Pool, several restaurants, fitness centre and spa.

Ritz Taipei

155 Minchuan East Road, Taipei. Tel. (02) 597 1234, fax (02) 596 9222

City centre (north). Luxurious prestige hotel, art deco interiors. Health centre, restaurants, conference facilities.

Riverview

77 Huanho South Road, Section 1, Taipei. Tel. (02) 311 3131, fax (02) 361 3737

City centre (west), on river. Restaurants, shops.

Santos

439 Chengteh Road, Taipei. Tel. (02) 596 3111, fax (02) 596 3120

City centre (north-west). Health club, restaurants, conference facilities.

Sherwood

637 Minsheng East Road, Taipei. Tel. (02) 718 1188, fax (02) 713 0707

City centre (north-east). Pool, fitness centre, restaurants, conference facilities.

Taipei Fortuna

122 Chungshan North Road, Section 2, Taipei. Tel. (02) 563 1111, fax (02) 561 9777

City centre (north). Health club, restaurants.

Taipei Miramar ▌▌
420 Minchuan East Road, Taipei. Tel. (02) 505 3456, fax (02) 502 9173
City centre (north-east). Large hotel, garden setting. Pool, restaurants,
conference facilities.

Taipei YMCA International ▌
19 Hsuchang Street, Taipei. Tel. (02) 311 3201, fax (02) 311 3209
City centre, near railway station. Small block. Restaurant.

United ▌▌
200 Kuangfu South Road, Taipei. Tel. (02) 773 1515, fax (02) 741 2789
City centre (east). Glass tower. Restaurants, conference facilities.

Near Taipei

CKS Airport Hotel ▌▌
*P.O. Box 66, Chiang Kai-shek International Airport, Taoyuan.
Tel. (03) 383 3666, fax (03) 383 3546*
Large, modern airport hotel. Pool, tennis, restaurants, convention
facilities.

Chinatrust Hsinchu ▌▌
106 Chungyang Road, Hsinchu. Tel. (035) 263181, fax (035) 269244
In centre of university city, 62 km. (39 mi.) south-west of Taipei.
Restaurants.

China Yangmingshan ▌▌
237 Kochih Road, Yangmingshan. Tel. (02) 861 6661, fax (02) 861 3885
Small resort hotel in garden setting on north-eastern outskirts of Taipei.
Health facilities, hot spring, pool, tennis.

Communication Palace ▌
30 Yuya Road, Peitou, Taipei. Tel. (02) 891 3031, fax (02) 891 5461
In spa town in northern suburbs of Taipei. Pool, hot spring, restaurant.

Kodak Keelung ▌
7 Yee 1 Road, Keelung. Tel. (02) 423 0111, fax (02) 425 2233
In centre of Keelung. Quite small hotel, restaurant.

Lucky Star ▌
*8 Lane 24, Tehyang Road, Chiaochi Hsiang, Ilan. Tel. (039) 881110,
fax (039) 881114*
Close to Chiaochi Hsiang railway station. Near east coast, 50 km. (31 mi.)
south-east of Taipei.

Taoyuan Plaza

151 Fuhsing Road, Taoyuan. Tel. (03) 337 9222, fax (03) 337 9250
Central Taoyuan, near CKS International Airport, west of Taipei.
Restaurants.

East Coast

Chinatrust Hualien

2 Yongshing Road, Hualien. Tel. (038) 221171, fax (038) 221185
Close to sea and city. Pool, gardens, restaurant, conference facilities. Ami
aboriginal group welcomes guests.

Jyh-Been (Chihpen)

5 Lungchuan, Chihpen, Taitung. Tel. (089) 512 220, fax (089) 513067
In old, established resort, about 16 km. (10 mi.) south-west of Taitung.
Hot springs feed large pools. Restaurant, disco.

Marshal

36 Kungyuan Road, Hualien. Tel. (038) 326123, fax (038) 326140
City centre, near sea. Pool, restaurants.

Tienhsiang Lodge

Tienhsiang, Hualien. Tel. (038) 691155, fax (038) 691160
Rustic retreat at inland end of the Taroko Gorge. Pool, garden, restaurant.

Central and Western Taiwan

Alishan House

3 West Alishan, Shanglin Village, Alishan Hsiang, Chiayi.
Tel. (05) 267 9811, fax (05) 267 9596
Resort hotel in Alishan forest reserve. Restaurant. Separate rustic part at
upper railway station, made from old carriages.

Chinatrust Sun Moon Lake

23 Chungcheng Road, Sun Moon Lake, Nantou. Tel. (049) 855911,
fax (049) 855268
Resort on Sun Moon Lake. Pool, tennis, golf, restaurant.

Dragon Valley

138 Tongkuan Road, Section 1, Kukuan, Taichung. Tel. (045) 951325,
fax (045) 951226
Hot-spring resort hotel near entrance to valley and waterfalls. Restaurants,
conference facilities.

Gallant

257 Wenhua Road, Chiayi. Tel. (05) 223 5366, fax (05) 223 9522
Modern block near city centre and railway station. Pool, restaurants.

Grandhill Cottage

Kuantzuling. Tel. (06) 682 2500, fax (06) 6822304
Modern chalet-style hotel/motel in old, established hill resort. Lovely views from hilltop site. Restaurant.

Green Mountain

56-5 Tsaoling Village, Kukeng County, Yunlin. Tel. (055) 831201
Large, functional hotel in expanding resort area of forests and waterfalls. Gardens, restaurant.

Lishan Guest House

Lishan. Tel. (045) 989501, fax (045) 989505
Resort hotel on East-West Cross Island Highway. Pool, restaurants.

Plaza International

431 Taya Road, Taichung. Tel. (04) 295 6789, fax (04) 293 0099
Modern tower, north-west of city centre. Pool, health centre, restaurants, conference facilities.

Sun Link Sea

23-6 Chungcheng Road, Luku, Nantou. Tel. (049) 612211,
fax (049) 612216, reservation number in Taipei (02) 721 9169
Resort hotel in Shanlinhsi ("Sun Link Sea") forest reserve. Restaurant.

Taichung Park International

17 Kungyuan Road, Taichung. Tel. (04) 220 5181, fax (04) 222 5757
Near city centre and park. Restaurants.

Wuling Guest House

Wuling Farm, Lishan. Tel. (045) 901183
Resort hotel in woodland, near East-West Highway. Restaurant.

Southern Taiwan

Caesar Park

6 Kenting Road, Hengchun Town, Pingtung Hsien. Tel. (08) 886 1888,
fax (08) 886 1818
Resort hotel near beach in Kenting National Park. Gardens, pool, health club, tennis, sailing, diving. Restaurants, disco.

Grand ▐▐
Chengching Lake, Kaohsiung. Tel. (07) 383 5911, fax (07) 381 4889
Chinese palace-style hotel 6 km. (4 mi.) east of city. Pool, restaurants, conference facilities.

Holiday Garden ▐▐
279 Liuho 2nd Road, Kaohsiung. Tel. (07) 241 0121, fax (07) 251 2000
City centre, near river. Garden setting. Pool, health club, restaurants, shops, conference facilities.

Kenting House ▐
101 Park Road, Kenting, Hengchung, Pingtung. Tel. (08) 886 1370, reservations (08) 886 1379, fax (08) 886 1377
Resort hotel in garden setting in Kenting National Park. Plainer annexe and beach houses by the sea. Pools, restaurants.

OK Hill ▐
50 Sail Rock Road, Kenting, Hengchun Town, Pingtung Hsien. Tel. (08) 886 1601, fax (08) 886 1366
Resort hotel near beach in Kenting National Park. Pool, fitness centre, restaurants, conference facilities.

Redhill ▐
46 Chengkung Road, Tainan. Tel. (06) 225 8121, fax (06) 221 6711
Modern city-centre hotel. Restaurants.

Tainan ▐▐
1 Chengkung Road, Tainan. Tel. (06) 228 9101, fax (06) 226 8502
Elegant, modernized hotel across main square from railway station. Pool, restaurants.

Penghu (The Pescadores)

Chang Chun ▐
8 Chungcheng Road, Makung. Tel. (069) 273336
Small hotel in town centre, near harbour. Restaurant.

Pao Hwa ▐
2 Chungcheng Road, Makung. Tel. (069) 274881
Compact hotel in town centre, near harbour. Restaurant.

peak and the highest in north-east Asia. It's not a tough climb: in fact there's a path all the way, and a statue of a climbing politician on the top. Local experts say you just need two days, warm and waterproof clothing, food and water reserves and advice about routes. For this and any other expedition off the beaten track in the mountains, you may need a special pass (see p. 111) and for serious climbs you must go in groups of three or more.

For the less energetic, one of the best engineered new highways on the island connects Alishan and **Tungpu**. A hotsprings resort in the Yushan National Park, this little town is the centre of a network of mountain paths originally made by the aboriginal people of the region centuries ago. Some of them are not for anyone liable to vertigo as they take direct routes across cliff faces. Unfortunately, when cut by rock falls they aren't repaired with the same diligence as the roads.

If you are travelling independently, there's no need to return to Alishan. You can continue to Shuili and on to Sun Moon Lake (see p. 59) in a memorable mountain circuit.

Top Temples

North-west of Chiayi, **Peikang** is the home of the most important, most active and richest of Taiwan's temples dedicated to Matsu, Goddess of the Sea. According to legend, she was born in 960 on an island off the coast of Fukien. As a child, she saved her brothers' lives by calming the sea and this, along with other miracles, caused her to be venerated as a goddess after she died at the young age of 28. Her birthday is celebrated on the 23rd day of the 3rd lunar month (late April to early May) with the biggest explosion of enthusiasm imaginable, here at Peikang. Tens, perhaps hundreds of thousands of people converge on the town; an inferno of firecrackers threatens the eardrums; whole percussion orchestras of drums, bells and cymbals sound through cumulus clouds of incense smoke; shamans cut themselves until the blood runs, and processions carrying giant images parade through the streets.

If you don't happen to coincide with any special event, you'll at least be able to take a more leisurely look at the temple itself, with its exuberant soaring roof of tangled, rainbow-coloured statuary.

Every day of the month which ends in a 3, 6 or 9, Peikang holds its traditional **water-buffalo market**. As agriculture modernizes, tractors of all sizes are taking the place of draught animals, but not so long ago, their pulling power, milk, manure, meat and leather were indispensable. Then, most towns had "ox markets": now this is one of the few left, and the largest. The action starts early—soon after dawn—with noisy bargaining and tests of the animals' strength. The winners are decorated with a new harness: losers may end up on the butcher's slab.

In the foothills on the road up to Alishan, 12 kilometres (7 mi.) east of Chiayi, **Wufeng Temple** honours the self-sacrifice of an 18th-century negotiator who was trusted by the head-hunting aboriginal tribe in the area. He told them they could take one more head, and that would be their last, if they waited in a certain place at an appointed time. A hooded man approached, and was duly despatched. But the victim was then found to be the negotiator himself. Tradition says that the tribe was shocked into giving up head-hunting from that moment. The temple is alive with birds, and some of its rooms house a museum of statues and paintings depicting Wufeng and the aboriginal people and displays of their artefacts.

You'll get the feeling that the earth's crust is especially thin in Taiwan: there are so many hot springs. In a steep-sided valley just off Route 3 and south of Wufeng Temple, **Kuantzuling** is an old-established resort and the lower town has a neglected look. But uphill, past an imaginative new chalet-style "motel", a short drive or an hour's walking will bring you to something special. At **Water-Fire Crevice**, hot water and burning gases spurt out of the ground at the same spot, so flames flicker over the bubbling surface. The site is practically in someone's back garden, but the family will give you a friendly welcome. In the Kuantzuling area, you can make a circuit of various monasteries and temples set amid pleasant woods and hills.

Both a rough logging road from Kuantzuling and the inland scenic route south from Chiayi which it joins lead to **Tsengwen Reservoir.** Otherwise, it's a 60-kilometre (37-mi.) excursion north-east from Tainan. Since a dam and hydroelectric scheme were finished in 1973 it has become

Taiwan's biggest lake, set rather beautifully in a steep wooded valley. The outflow from Tsengwen is sent through a tunnel to **Coral Lake** (*Wu-shantou*) lower down on the edge of the coastal plain, in a strange eroded landscape of little hills and valleys.

THE SOUTH-WEST

You're truly in the tropics here, sheltered by mountains from the north-east monsoon, enjoying warm, dry winters—and paying back a little in summer when south-west winds bring wet spells. There's as much to see as anywhere in Taiwan and some special ingredients. Historic Tainan has a relaxed, almost Mediterranean feeling; Kaohsiung is an industrial powerhouse; the southern mountains are the best place to look for traditional aboriginal culture; and Kenting is a fully fledged beach resort.

Tainan

First a Dutch fort and trading post, then the headquarters of the Ming loyalist Koxinga and his successors from 1663 to 1683, and the island's capital until 1887, Tainan still claims

cultural seniority. And religious pre-eminence: it's been called the "City of 100 Temples". Of course, such names are usually not to be taken literally. But the difference this time is that the label is an understatement: there are over 200.

Each of Taiwan's cities has its own pace and flavour. People in Tainan seem to have more time and the high proportion of students here may account for the greater use and comprehension of English.

We don't suggest that you try to see more than a sprinkling of temples and shrines, but walking round the city looking for them is a pleasure and an adventure—there's something surprising round every corner. The main hotels give out a useful bilingual street map marking some of the important sites. Orient yourself—the semicircular plaza in front of the main railway station is a good focus—and set off. Running west and away from the station is Chengkung Road.

Chihkan Towers (212 Min-tsu Road) stand where a fort was built by the Dutch in 1653. Called Providentia (or Provintia—early maps disagree), it was intended to control the turbulent town facing their offshore stronghold,

Zeelandia. The fort's surrender to Koxinga in 1661 led to the final defeat of the Dutch the following year. The towers you see now are a 19th-century construction, decorative rather than defensive. Inside, paintings and displays commemorate Koxinga's victory: one model shows the Dutch buildings, which wouldn't look out of place beside an Amsterdam canal.

The **Wu** ("Warrior") **Temple**, dedicated to the martial hero Kuankung, stands on the opposite side of the road from Chihkan Towers, although the entrance is down a side street (Yungfu Road). The interior is sombre, with fine 18th-century carved ceilings. Nearby, reached by an alleyway, the colourful, incense-laden **Matsu Temple** is even earlier, dating from 1683, when the successful Manchu expedition wanted to thank the Sea Goddess for their safe voyage. While you're in this part of the city, don't hesitate to dive down the narrow alleys and explore. There's almost a village atmosphere, and every tiny workshop and every home seems to have its ancestral shrine.

The handsome green-tiled **Koxinga Shrine** (Kaishan Road) was built in 1875 with the approval of the Ching emperor, successor to the Manchu, thus implying posthumous forgiveness of the Ming hero, their former arch-enemy. Koxinga has never been deified, though many have regarded him as divine. Here, he is shown as an impressive seated figure in the main hall. In the same garden compound as the shrine, the **museum** is worth seeing for its collections of early furniture, costume and prehistory section.

The **Confucian Temple** (2 Nanmen Road) dates originally from 1665, soon after the expulsion of the Dutch. That makes it Taiwan's oldest, and with its delicately curved roofs, elegant halls and quiet courtyards, now beautifully restored, it is often said to be the finest.

South near the city's sports stadium, the bright, massive Buddhist **Chuhsi Temple** has two great white elephants standing guard while children race electric cars on the forecourt. For contrast, stroll over to the pretty little **Five Concubines Temple** in the same park

Money to burn:
it's only "ghost money",
but it will ensure
a smooth passage for the dead
on their journey to heaven.

area. On the way back to the centre, you'll pass **Tananmen** gate, one of several restored vestiges of the old city walls.

Tainan has a substantial Christian minority, and if you look into the **church** on Chienkuo Road you'll see a remarkable interior with a lot in common with Confucian temple art. In the same street, an obscure doorway opens into a different world, the **East Mountain Temple**, its crowded little halls and narrow passages so full of smoke that your eyes stream.

That, your tired legs may say, is enough temple-touring for one day. Let Tainan's restaurants revive you: an endless choice is scattered all over the city, but especially in the area behind the railway station. Night markets are mostly to be found north of the centre beyond Chungshan Park.

Near Tainan

West of the city, a few kilometres away, the suburb of **Anping** seems designated for leisure development, with motels, sports facilities, a wax museum, fairground rides and the beach not far away. Holiday craft have joined fishing boats in the creeks which cut through

the flat landscape. And visitors also come to see what's left of two contrasting castles.

When the Dutch built **Fort Zeelandia** in 1623, they chose a spit of land, almost an island, which their ships could help to defend. The coast has silted up so much since then that the sea has retreated out of sight. One red-brick wall of the original fort still stands, with the multiple tentacles of a banyan tree clinging to it in mutual support. The terraced villa next to it dates from the Japanese era and the rocket-shaped observation tower is still more recent.

Not far away, but so low-lying it's hard to spot, **Yitsai Chin Cheng** (Eternal Castle) was built to a French design in 1875, to deter foreign—especially Japanese—naval threats to Tainan. The massive walls and deep ditch remain, and some huge cannon. You can walk right round the ramparts but, like Zeelandia, the fort is now some distance from the sea.

So too, is Koxinga's landing site, **Luerhmen** (Deer's Ear Gate), a 20-minute drive north of Tainan, where an utterly featureless landscape seems to have inspired temple-builders to vaulting ambition. Rising like a mirage from the mudflats, rice paddies and fish-farms, the palatial **Holy Mother Temple** complex is Taiwan's biggest. Impressive in the misty distance, it's magnificent close up. The Matsu cult, Taoism and Buddhism are combined in what even the tourism authorities cheerfully call a "one-stop religious centre". Outside, a funfair and market stalls supplement the attractions.

Not far away, the **Matsu Temple** (Heaven Queen Temple) at Luerhmen is the home of a precious 1,000-year-old figure of the goddess which Koxinga himself brought to Taiwan. Not to be outdone, it has undergone a grandiose expansion, surrounding itself with a riot of colour and carving.

Believe it or not, this still leaves perhaps the most important temple in the region to visit, if you have the time and stamina. Another half-hour's drive to the north, through salt-pans and fish-farms, **Nankunshen Temple** (or Peimen Temple, after the adjoining town) dates from 1662. When it's quiet, you can look at leisure at the shrine halls, honouring five martial heroes, Kuanyin and the Emperor of Hell, and wander in the gardens where shrubs have been sculpted into bird and animal shapes. But when there's a ceremony, it will seem as if half the island has come, armed with gongs and fireworks.

Kaohsiung

Few old maps show the fishing village which was to grow into the third busiest container port in the world (after Rotterdam and Hong Kong). To continue the list of global superlatives, it has the second largest dry dock, and it's the biggest ship-scrapper. The population has exploded to over 1.3 million. If the statistics take your breath away, so may the atmosphere. For Kaohsiung is the centre of Taiwan's heavy industry—petrochemicals, cement, steel—and a penalty has been paid in pollution. On a bad day, your eyes will run and your nose tingle. Many people wear smog masks. The good news is that the worst emitters have been moved away from the centre, whose wide streets can let fresher air circulate.

Kaohsiung is easy to reach. It has Taiwan's second international airport with plenty of domestic flights as well, it's the southern end of the toll highway from Taipei and the north coast, and there are frequent trains.

Several big hotels are on or near the Aiho (Love River), less noxious since an expensive clean-up campaign, though you'd still want to avoid falling in. Like Taipei, there's no single focal point or city centre. You'll find most shops and entertainment spread across an area roughly bounded by Chienkuo and Wufu roads, from the noisier bars west of Love River near the port to the Cultural Centre at the eastern end. The north–south artery here is Chungshan Road. Part of Liuho Road (Section 2) is closed to traffic every evening and turns into a **night market**, with the usual stalls and fairground games and several superb fish restaurants.

Near Kaohsiung

The various sights are scattered far and wide: you might do well to take a couple of half-day tours. West of the city, a steep hill called **Wanshoushan** (Longevity Mountain) is topped by the impressive Martyrs' Shrine, but it's only worth the

Straight into the jaws of the dragon—it's the lucky way to enter the pagodas at Lotus Lake.

climb on a clear day for the view. At **Hsitzuwan**, west of Wanshoushan, the sea is as crowded in summer as the beach.

Ferries or a road tunnel will take you across to **Chichin**, the long thin island protecting Kaohsiung harbour and said to be where the first immigrants from the mainland settled. Seafood restaurants and the beach on the seaward side are the main attractions.

The huge ship-breaking operations, steelworks and shipbuilders are all some way south of the city centre, beyond the airport. (Visits are normally possible only for those with some official business there.)

A short drive north of the city past a restored town gate brings you to **Lotus Lake**, site of three remarkable constructions. The exuberant seven-tier **Dragon and Tiger Pagodas**, built out in the lake and reached by a zigzag bridge, are like something from a fun park. Go in through the dragon's mouth, not the tiger's—that could bring bad luck, though it's all right to exit that way. A short walk away along the lake shore, the **Spring and Autumn Pavilion** is entered through another dragon: a causeway leads to a delicate fantasy of curved

73

golden roofs and red columns. Much more restrained, the new **Confucian Shrine** (1976) in strictly traditional style stands in huge grounds.

Chengching Lake and park on the north-western outskirts of Kaohsiung make another favourite place of escape. If you've come from Taipei, you'll recognize the palace style of the Grand Hotel. You can hire a boat to go on the lake, take the road round its shore to the Chunghsing (Restoration) Pagoda and Nine-Turn Bridge, or play golf on the tree-lined course.

In an ingenious form of crop rotation, some broad ponds near the lake are used for fish-farming for half the year, and as rice-paddies for the other half. At one surprising sort of "farm", female fresh-water clams are artificially stimulated into producing lustrous pearls: you'll find pretty necklaces and earrings in the showrooms.

Excursions from Kaohsiung

Fokuangshan (Light of Buddha Mountain) lies in the hills about an hour's drive to the north-east of Kaohsiung. A giant, 32-metre-high (105-ft.) gold-coloured concrete Buddha towers above no fewer than 480 small (well, life-size) replicas. Nearby in beautifully tended grounds stand vast and impressive shrine-halls, one with three great statues of the seated figure of Buddha, another with a standing figure, in white as usual, of Kuanyin.

Other buildings scattered in the gardens and wooded slopes include accommodation for pilgrims and visiting scholars—this foundation takes a leading role in the post-World War II revival of a purer form of Buddhism in Taiwan. For a bizarre experience, meander through **Pure Land Cave**, a huge artificial grotto filled with plaster models and mechanical figures.

North of here, a group of attractions draws car loads of people out of Kaohsiung at weekends: **Akungtien Reservoir**, hot-spring pools at **Kangshan**, weird rock formations publicized as **Moon World**, and **Butterfly Valley** near the town of Meinung, which itself is famous for the

Giant gilded statue of Buddha watches benignly over Fokuangshan amid hundreds of smaller replicas.

FISHERMEN'S ISLANDS

Scattered halfway between Taiwan and the Chinese mainland, 64 islands and islets make up the Penghu archipelago. The biggest, also called Penghu, is home to half of the 120,000 population, and most of them live in the only large town, Makung.

The old Portuguese name, the Pescadores, means "Fishermen's Islands", and fishing is still the major occupation. Farmers here have a tough row to hoe: if you fly in you'll see a maze of stone walls protecting little fields of sweet potatoes, peanuts, melons and sorghum from winter gales and salt spray.

Makung's attractions are its harbour and fishing boats, seafood restaurants and the oldest of many temples dedicated to Matsu. Bridges and causeways link the three largest islands and a couple of smaller ones. The **Penghu Bay Bridge,** joining the main island with Paisha (White Sand) and Hsiyu (West Island), is Taiwan's longest at 5 1/2 kilometres (3 1/2 mi.). If you aren't with a group, negotiate a rate for a tour by taxi or rent a scooter to explore the varied coastline. Rocky coves and caves, cliffs and natural arches alternate with white sandy beaches where the swimming and snorkelling are superb.

There's no problem getting to Penghu, with several flights a day from Kaohsiung and other west coast cities as well as from Taipei. Some tour companies even sell day excursions. Ferries sail from Kaohsiung and although the four-hour voyage can be rough in winter, it's a popular summer cruise. (Other ships make the trip from Putai and Taichung.)

making of traditional oiled-paper umbrellas.

Maolin in the foothills is a Rukai aboriginal tribal village, reached by a gateway where you buy an entry ticket and get a mountain pass. The village itself is not remarkable, but a short distance up the road, the valley has been designated as a recreation area. A 40-minute walk up steep bamboo-covered slopes brings you to the scenic Maolin Valley waterfall. Back on the road, and 12 kilometres (7 mi.) further on in **Tona** village, some of the Rukai still live in traditional slate-walled, slate-roofed houses.

To the south, **Santimen** (Three Way Gate) marks the beginning of Paiwan tribal lands. Many of the townspeople are Paiwan and the shops sell mountain products from tea to deer horn. But to see traditional Paiwan life, you'll have to travel further into the mountains—and for that you'll need a pass from the police. There's an easy way to see tribal art and architecture, and that is to head for the nearby **Taiwan Aboriginal Culture Park.** Here, along a steep winding valley, each of the tribes living in Taiwan is represented by a separate small village with examples of its building styles. Some are replicas, some have been brought here from their original sites and reassembled. The park is more spread out than the older-established Formosan Aboriginal Culture Village near Sun Moon Lake (see p. 59) and the setting is more dramatic, but you may find less happening here. It makes sense to take a shuttle bus to the highest point and walk down.

South of Kaohsiung, at Lin-yuan or Tungkang harbours, you can escape on one of the frequent ferries to **Hsaio Liuchiu**, a rural little island less than 5 kilometres (3 mi.) long. A popular weekend excursion, the trip to its sheltered little harbour takes about 45 minutes.

THE SOUTHERN PENINSULA

If the map of Taiwan looks like a leaf, this is its stalk. The first Chinese settlers, farmers from Fukien, called the peninsula Hengchun ("Eternal Spring")—with good reason. The sea is warm enough for swimming all year round, winters are dry, summers hot and showery.

Like most visitors, you'll probably head first for the resort of **Kenting** on its sheltered sandy bay, intent on relaxing on the beach, windsurfing or snorkelling over the coral. If you stay at one of the big holiday hotels, you can borrow their equipment as well as using their pools, gardens and various sports facilities.

When you're ready for a change, there's plenty of choice, and all kinds of transport available. Most of the coast, the mountains behind and the offshore waters here make up **Kenting National Park**, 326 square kilometres (126 sq. mi.) of extraordinary variety. A short distance inland from the small town of Kenting, call in at the park headquarters to collect a map and some of their excellent literature about the plants, animals and geology of the region. Further up the hill, the Forest Recreation Area was founded as a botanic garden in 1906: over 1,200 species are labelled with their English, Latin and Chinese names.

The skyline is dominated by a tall, needle-sharp rocky peak—and that's more or less what its name, **Tachienshih-shan,** means. It's 318 metres (1,043 ft.) high and getting up it requires a strenuous walk and scramble, but not a severe climb, and the view from the top is superb. You start off near the park headquarters, where they can advise on routes. One of the sights from the peak, **Lungluan Lake**, is an objective for bird-watchers. Just north of it, **Hengchun** is the only place in Taiwan to have kept a large part of its wall and gates.

The south-western cape, **Maopitou** (Cat Nose Tip), is a sharply eroded mass of ancient coral, with good fishing and diving from the rocky shore below, and views of the bay—and the concrete domes of its nuclear power station. The longer south-eastern headland ends at **Oluanpi** (Goose Beak), topped by a lighthouse built in 1882 after numerous tragic shipwrecks. The cliffs look down on a strangely convoluted coral shoreline: divers and snorkellers rate these waters as among the best for colourful marine life.

Kenting is about as far from Taipei as you can get without taking to the water. And you'll want to do that too.

WHAT TO DO

SPORTS AND PASTIMES

The day begins early for Taiwan's countless keep-fit enthusiasts. You can join them in the parks and gardens and you'll even see them outside their front doors, some performing *tai chi*, like slow-motion shadow boxing, others disco-dancing to music from a ghetto-blaster. Both sexes and all ages from toddlers to grandparents get involved. Like most activities, the Chinese think exercise is better in a group, so classes at health clubs have caught on.

Many hotels have opened elaborate fitness centres, and a few have jogging tracks, although any kind of running is more pleasurable away from city smogs. You'll find some hotels in Taipei and elsewhere with **tennis** and one or two with **squash** courts, or you may be able to play at public courts and local clubs.

If you haven't brought your racket or you need some new sportswear, this could be a good place to buy—Taiwan is a major producer.

The first **golf** course on the island, the Taiwan Golf and Country Club at Tamsui traces its origins to 1919. Now there are more than 25, almost all in the north and west, and it's claimed that 300,000 people play. You may be able to arrange a game through your hotel or certain travel agencies, particularly if you can play on a weekday. Japanese groups come on special golf tours, and it's a good idea to try to start very early in the day to avoid being caught behind a log jam of players. The weather's better too, most mornings.

Those big wire cages alongside factories, farms and houses may be golf driving ranges, but take a closer look. You'll find many of them actually contain an automatic pitcher—more like a cannon—so you can practise your **baseball** shots. The game itself is one of America's most successful exports to Taiwan.

When city streets do their summer imitation of a sauna, **swimming** is a tempting way to cool off. A few hotels have pools, and some sort of beach is never too far away, though Sunday traffic can prolong the process of getting there. Taipei people head for the sandy bays of the north (Paishawan, Chinshan and Green Bay) and the north-east (especially Fulung and Yenliao). Kaohsiung's own beaches are conveniently near the city but neither the shore nor the water can be guaranteed pristine clean. The purer environment of the island's only year-round resort, Kenting, is a couple of hours' drive south.

The coral-encrusted coasts of north-eastern and southern Taiwan are rich in fish and fine for **snorkelling**. Clubs and some hotels may be able to lend you masks and goggles. **Scuba diving** is organized through the China Diving Association (tel. 02-596 2341).

Colourful **sailboards** flutter across the water in dozens at the busier beaches: you can rent them by the hour. Jet-skis are catching on—and efforts are being made to keep them away from swimming areas.

You might like the idea of shooting rapids in a rubber boat: several companies now organize **river-rafting** down the Hsiukuluan, south of Hualien (see p. 42). Otherwise, make gentler progress by hiring a boat and **rowing** on one of the scenic lakes or reservoirs.

There isn't much they don't know about **fishing** on Taiwan and the smaller islands. You can join a host of local enthusiasts casting from the rocky shores of the north and east, or pay a fee to hold your rod over a fish-farm's pond. If you are after bigger game and want to go deep-sea sport-fishing, you'll need to arrange it in advance through the R.O.C. Fishing Association (tel. 02-511 1022). They should be able to advise you about the necessary licence, which you'll have to obtain from the police.

Hiking and Climbing

More than half of Taiwan is covered by mountains, with dozens of peaks over 3,000 metres (almost 10,000 ft.). In climbing terms, few are very difficult: many just involve more or less strenuous walking. The Chinese love dramatic scenery, and groups head for the hills every weekend.

Hostels have been strategically placed on the way to a few famous summits, where routes are well marked and even "improved" with wooden paths and steps. For most high-altitude objectives, you'll have to plan a two- or three-day expedition and get a permit from the Alpine Association (10F, 185 Chungshan N. Road Section 2, Taipei). They can also advise you about guides and the passes needed for some areas and obtained from the police (see p. 111). Be prepared for drenching rain, and for bitter cold. Snowfalls in mid-winter allow Taiwan's **skiing** fans to hit the slopes of Hohuanshan (see p. 58).

SHOPPING

If you're part of the "Born to Shop" brigade, welcome to Taiwan. Most of the population are your fellow members, jamming stores and markets every day and evening: the rest are equally dedicated to selling. From giant department stores to street vendors with just one kind of plastic toy, the choice is daunting.

Forget any preconceived ideas about rock-bottom prices, fake brand-names and shoddy goods. Since the New Taiwan dollar (NT$) was uncoupled from the US dollar, it's risen and taken price equivalents with it. Bargains can be found but you'll need to be selective and compare prices. The authorities and manufacturers' organizations have cracked down on counterfeiting, and though there are still some false "designer" clothes on street stalls they're not seriously expected to fool anyone. Increasingly, factories are turning to quality goods and high technology.

Where to Shop

Each sub-centre of Taipei has its **department stores**: west of the main railway station, up Chungshan North Road, and eastwards on Chunghsiao East and Nanking East roads. Kaohsiung and Taichung, not to be outdone, have several giants, with other cities following suit. On the plus side, the stores take credit cards, display prices, imply a certain guarantee of quality, offer a huge selection and one-stop shopping (including food malls and often a supermarket)—and they're air-conditioned. But signs in anything but Chinese are rare. You may end up confused and frustrated. And you can't haggle over the price—which may be a relief.

83

Try the **small shops** as well. They often undercut the big stores, or they'll give discounts for cash, if you're the first customer of the day, or for some other reason. Always ask. The same applies with the myriad **street traders**. If you have no common language, they'll write down the price asked and you can counter with what you offer. Much quicker is the simple sign language everyone here uses for numbers: ask any local contact to teach you.

What to Buy

Clothing fills endless racks in the stores and covers market stalls. Top designers from Europe, the U.S. and Japan have clothes made here and you'll see their "in-house" boutiques in the department stores. It can be difficult to find large sizes, but there'll be no such problem if you have something custom-made. Tailors offer to complete a suit or a dress in 24 hours. Casual and sportswear and **children's clothes** can be good buys.

Experience a spell of wet weather in Taiwan and you'll understand why they're so good at making **rainwear**. Look for **leather** clothing and accessories, mass-produced or hand-tooled, snakeskin and a host of lookalike synthetics. Taiwan is a major producer of shoes, including famous-name sports shoes.

The latest **toys** are made here, including a lot of entertaining gimmicks and gadgets. Among the electronic marvels for adults, films on laser-disc are all the rage.

Traditional crafts are probably your best bet for souvenirs and presents. Look for decorative **knot-tying**, an ancient and intriguing art. Pillows, pictures and purses are embellished with fine **embroidery**, some of it in gold thread.

As a perfect image of old China, **oiled paper umbrellas** look enchanting, and they work too, though you wouldn't want to risk raising one in a high wind. Painted paper **lanterns** can be subtle or dazzling, and if you buy the kind which fold flat they're easily packed. And if your eye is taken by rich, heavy **furniture** in carved rosewood, sandalwood or teak, or the lighter bamboo and rattan, the traders will gladly ship it for you. Naturally, they're

Old crafts don't die. They live on at the Formosan Aboriginal Culture Village, near Sun Moon Lake.

well versed in your country's import regulations.

The top end of the **jade** business is a minefield which only connoisseurs can safely navigate. Novices could begin their education at Taipei's Saturday and Sunday jade market, held in the shadow of the Chienkuo South Road/Jenai Road overpass. The less-prized dark green jade is found in Taiwan, and other local **semi-precious stones** include serpentine and agate. Salmon-pink, white and red **corals** are made into necklaces and earrings. They're reasonably priced, and so are the attractively uneven but lustrous **fresh-water pearls**.

Centuries-old crafts continue: look for **cloisonné enamel**, and metalwork, especially decorative **brass** where the supply has been greatly boosted by the quantities salvaged when old ships are scrapped. **Ceramics**, of course, are synonymous with China. You can buy fine reproductions of treasures you'll see in the National Palace Museum—there's no stigma attached to copying masterpieces—and visit the potteries in Peitou and Miaoli which make everything from huge vases to tiny porcelain teacups.

Landscape **paintings** of mountains, trees and water have a controlled gravity. Westerners may prefer the brilliant appeal of bird, animal and flower pictures. There's no end to the variety of less serious souvenirs: butterfly-wing collages, fans, masks, carved cowrie shells and dough sculptures, baked and painted.

The non-profit Chinese Handicraft Mart at 1 Hsuchou Road, Taipei has a wide selection, at fixed prices, but if you think you can haggle your way to a better bargain, try the crowded "China Bazaar" along Chunghua Road. Don't assume that "antiques" are all they seem, or exactly what the vendor tells you—many ancient skills are still very much alive today.

Just off the expressway north of Taichung, the town of Sanyi seems entirely devoted to carving delicate **wood sculptures**—birds, pagodas and mythical figures, some of them seeming to grow out of the natural lines of the wood.

When they want something special, Taiwan people like to go to the source or buy from actual makers, sure that they can get a better price and a fresher or more authentic product. So they'll buy sacks of dried mushrooms and packets of sliced deer horn in mountain villages. **Honey** and that panacea, **royal jelly**, come from the beekeeping areas east of Kaohsiung. Connoisseurs head for the tea plantations to buy green, black and especially oolong **teas**. The price range is enormous—starting high and going on up to prized varieties that really do cost more than their weight in gold.

You may have to get visiting cards printed (see p. 110) and if you're staying for a while, you might come to need a **chop**, a little hand-carved seal for putting your personal stamp—always in red—on documents. In any case, it's a great souvenir and there are plenty of street-corner chopmakers ready to do the job quickly. They'll devise a decorative Chinese version of your name (find a local linguist to check it, if you can) and carve it in bamboo for a small sum. The wealthy of course prefer jade or gold.

ENTERTAINMENT

After you've strolled through the night-market scene, stopping now and then to try your skill at throwing darts or firing popguns, what then? Countless flashing signs beckon, and some you can read, if not understand.

Venues vary from plush, with hostesses and very expensive drinks, to seedy—possibly also with hostesses and very expensive drinks. Unless you're with local contacts who know the

HIGH DRAMA

Chinese opera plots are simple. Good versus evil; boy meets girl—loses girl—finds girl again; virtue triumphant—after many a trial. Elaborate conventions have developed over a thousand years. Facial make-up conveys character (red for upstanding generals, black for fearless warriors, green for ghosts and evil spirits, multicoloured for rogues). No fewer than 18 kinds of beard signal different ages, ranks and occupations.

There are few props: actors show by gestures when they are opening a door, or entering a room (stepping over a high imaginary threshhold). Four men carrying flags symbolize a whole army; a man carrying a lantern shows that night has fallen. Costume colours tell more of the story: an emperor's robes are yellow, good people of high rank wear green, usurpers and barbarian generals are in crimson. With all these clues, and actors trained from childhood, the merest flick of a sleeve can be worth a page of dialogue.

score you'd do well to check on prices before you get started, in any kind of bar, dance hall or club. Don't be deterred from trying Taipei's nightlife, but make sure you know what you're getting into. No one will mind if you ask.

Some of the Western-style **pubs** put on weekend entertainment and the big **hotels** try to keep their guests indoors and attract some others too. Their discos, nightclubs and piano bars may stay open later than the typical midnight closing time outside.

"KTV" seems to be everywhere, and if you want to do your Sinatra or Streisand impersonation, this is for you. When the Japanese *karaoke* fad first arrived here it was called Kala-OK (you'll still see that sign too). Then the well-oiled executive songsters and other would-be vocalists were put on closed-circuit video. Hence KTV.

At **"MTV"** establishments you can rent a video movie and view it in a private room or a cubicle, depending on the size of your party. The biggest and flashiest places have bars, clubrooms and big-screen shows as well, and recent films on laserdisc. Some MTVs may be less respectable, but sin mostly

keeps a low profile in Taiwan, staying behind closed doors.

Films are hugely popular and cinemas show the very latest international releases, with the original soundtrack and Chinese subtitles added. (Some Chinese "martial arts" films may be subtitled in English). You can find the current schedules from Taipei's English-language daily newspapers. They'll also tell you what's on at the National Theater and National Concert Hall (at CKS Cultural Centre) and the Sun Yat-sen Memorial Hall, whether it's a touring rock band, string quartet or an opera.

Chinese opera looks and sounds like nothing else on earth. It's an unforgettable spectacle of gorgeous costumes, rainbow make-up, acrobatics, dance, battle scenes and melodrama. If the music sounds to your delicate Western ears like five different percussion-heavy orchestras tuning up, just wait for the falsetto shrieks of the singers. It's all highly stylized and emphatic, apparently because it evolved in tearooms where people paid less than full

In Chinese opera, every detail in the costume and shade in the make-up has a vital significance.

attention—which still happens in the slower passages.

You can try a short sample of Chinese opera as part of a "Taipei by Night" tour. If you intend to go the full distance, take advice so you can choose one of the more action-packed plots, or go with an expert who can explain the subtleties. Regular performances are put on at the Armed Forces Cultural Centre, 69 Chunghua Road Section 1, Taipei.

FESTIVALS

Stay more than a few days and chances are that you'll coincide with one of the dozens of celebrations that pepper the year. The big national holidays (see p. 113) usually mean a colourful parade in Taipei and other cities. Most religious festivals are decided by the lunar calendar, so their Gregorian-style dates vary from year to year. Check with the Taiwan Tourism Bureau and other publications for coming events. Here are the main ones:

Chinese New Year (late January or February). A time for family gatherings and visits, village processions and deafening infernos of firecrackers that go on for days—and nights.

Lantern Festival (February or early March). Fifteen days after Lunar New Year, massed lanterns in temples or carried in procession. Dragon and lion dances and Chinese opera. Tourism Week runs from three days before the festival to three days after.

Kuanyin's Birthday (March or early April). Processions at the many temples dedicated to the Goddess of Mercy, including Taipei's Lungshan Temple.

Matsu's Birthday (late April or May). Devotees flock to the hundreds of Matsu temples. Spectacular celebrations at Peikang, with maximum noise, smoke and crowds.

Dragon Boat Festival (late May or June). Ceremonies and races on waterways near the big cities.

Kuankung's Birthday (June). Worshippers throng the temples of the God of War, Righteousness and Brotherhood, including Taipei's Hsingtien Temple.

Birthday of City God (June). Stilt-walkers, dragon and lion dances.

Month of the Ghosts (August). Spirits are believed to be let out of Hades to roam the earth: people put food out and burn ghost money for them.

Mid-Autumn (Moon) Festival (September or early October). People gather to gaze at the moon in its brightest phase. Special round sweet "mooncakes" are served.

EATING OUT

Prepare for a gastronomic adventure. The tides of history combined to bring all the regional cuisines of mainland China to the island—which evolved its own styles too. Taiwan's climate, fertile soil and rich fishing grounds provide the finest ingredients. Add Chinese genius for the art of food, love of eating and the business acumen to set up restaurants and food stalls wherever people gather and you have a choice that can't be bettered anywhere.

For centuries, waves of settlers brought their culture and their cooking with them. Most came from China's southern coastal provinces, but others were exiles from all over the country, seeking sanctuary.

The Nationalists who crossed over in 1949–50 also came from every region of China. Cooks who had formerly worked for one family started their own restaurants and began to learn from each other. Later, the Cultural Revolution on the mainland tried to root out "bourgeois influences" including fine traditional cooking and some of its best exponents found refuge here.

When economic success brought general prosperity, everything was in place: the skills, the produce, the demand and the money. The result—a diner's paradise.

Choices

Gently flavoured but colourful and inventive **Cantonese** *(Kwangtung)* style is well known in the West but often in a debased form. Here, it's at its best. Stir-fried dishes, roast suckling pig and spring pigeon, deep-fried pastries, shark's-fin soup and abalone are among its specialities. Most of the big hotels in Taipei and many in the other cities and resorts have a Cantonese restaurant.

Fuchou cooking, from Fukien province, features even more seafood than Cantonese, similarly mild flavours and a wide variety of soups. Since

most early settlers came from Fukien, **Taiwanese** cuisine mainly evolved from their tradition, with even more abundant seafood, and liberal use of fresh herbs, especially coriander, ginger and garlic. Salted pork knuckle and feet, salt and dried fish and all sorts of other preserved foods are part of traditional Taiwan diet.

Far from the sea and the rice-growing regions, the western provinces are noted for hot and spicy dishes, sometimes fire-bombing your taste buds with chillies. **Szechuan** also uses fennel seed, ginger and coriander, and noodles or bread are preferred to rice. Marinated and smoked duck is an intriguingly flavoured speciality. **Hunan** food can be oilier but just as peppery-hot as Szechuan, or sweet-and-sour—the range is wide.

Although each northern province has its own cuisine, in Taiwan they tend to be grouped under the name of the historic capital, **Peking**. Wheat and corn are the local cereal crops, so noodles and steamed breads are staples. Meats are stewed, pan-fried and barbecued but the

From street stand to luxury restaurant, eating out in Taiwan is a treat for the taste buds.

best-known dish is Peking duck, dipped in a sweet syrup and dried, roasted in a special oven, carved in a particular way and served with pancakes, spring onions and a sweet sauce.

Shanghai refined the dishes of surrounding provinces into a rich and varied collection, rather oilier and heavier than southern coastal styles. Seafoods, steamed and stewed with generous seasoning and sauces, "beggar's chicken" (stuffed and baked in clay to trap all the juices), frogs' legs and crab are outstanding.

A **Mongolian barbecue** is a one-price, all-you-can-eat affair of meats, vegetables and sauces. You choose what you like, and hand it over to your assigned cook who speedily sizzles it on a large griddle. If you still have space, go round again. The **Korean** version of a barbecue *(bulgogi)* is cooked at the table, with plenty of ginger, red chilli paste, prodigious quantities of garlic and pickled vegetables.

The influence of Buddhism means that many people won't eat meat, so you'll find plenty of **vegetarian** restaurants and food stalls, often identified with the swastika symbol. Curiously, a lot of skill and effort is put into making imitation "meats", look-alikes of sliced roast pork, duck, chicken and sausage.

While you look around and try to decide where to eat, there's no need to go hungry. **Snacks** are a way of life: try the oyster pancakes, roast chestnuts, spring rolls, a whole baby octopus on a stick, peppery sausages, noodles, ears of sweetcorn, roasted or boiled. Chicken feet and duck necks are local favourites which may not appeal as much to Western tastes.

In the delicious little stuffed dumplings called **dim sum** (*tien hsin* in Mandarin) snacks reach the level of an art form—and a substantial lunch. Selections are wheeled round the dining room and you pick what you like. Hotel restaurants are likely to have someone to explain the choice: elsewhere you'll have to take a chance.

You don't need a word of Chinese, or much money, to eat at the informal **cafeterias** you'll find in the side streets of the cities. Just move along the counter, pointing at your choices (the cook will put them in a styrofoam tray). **Noodle-stalls** are another economical option, if you can explain what you want to go with your bowl of noodles. And if you're adept with chopsticks—noodles are

the big test. Don't hesitate to slurp: it's reckoned to enhance the flavour.

Traces remain from five decades of Japanese occupation, augmented today by the demands of Japanese visitors. So you'll find raw fish in *sushi* bars, lightly battered and deep-fried *tempura* dishes and steak or seafood *teppanyaki* (quickly cooked on a hot griddle). Fully-fledged **Japanese** restaurants with imported chefs are among the more expensive. And if you crave still more Asian alternatives, try **Vietnamese**, **Thai** or **Indonesian.**

Western-style **fast food** has caught on, with big-name hamburger and fried chicken franchises in every city. And Taipei can claim Mexican, Indian, Italian, French, German, Swiss and "English-pub" food too.

Probably the most eye-catching and mouthwatering of all are the amazing displays of **seafood** outside large or small restaurants or in the night markets. It's all as fresh as can be: much of the stock is kept live in holding tanks, behind the scenes or out front where you can point to the crawling crab or writhing eels that you fancy.

Don't assume that modest surroundings mean low prices. Seafood is never cheap: you can easily run up a bigger bill at a night market stall than you would have done in a top Taipei hotel. So make sure that the price of every item you order is written down, or you could be in for a nasty shock.

Breakfast in hotels often takes the form of a buffet, perhaps with Western, Chinese and Japanese favourite dishes. In small cafés the local version comprises fried dough, rice soup, warm soybean milk, augmented if you like by a fried-egg sandwich.

Taiwan's brilliant bakers make fresh breads, cakes and pastries galore for the bake shops, big stores and open-all-hours mini-markets (look for the "24" in their signs). It helps if your taste buds are flexible: you can't always tell by appearances whether the rolls are sweet or savoury.

Fruit lovers will be in heaven. Market stalls are laden, all year round, thanks to the varied climate and ingenious growers who stretch the seasons with the aid of greenhouses. Winter brings huge and luscious mandarins, pink and yellow grapefruit, tangy oranges, giant strawberries and sweet dates. Spring (February) is ushered in by loquats, knobbly "buddha-fruit" and the first

pineapples in a season that lasts until November. Plums, peaches and pears in early summer are followed by litchis and mangoes. Bananas, papayas and guavas are always available, along with one or other sort of melon.

Drinks

Naturally, all this fruit means delicious juices—not only orange and grapefruit, but peach, papaya, mango, guava and many more. Soft drinks based on all of these and more are sold in every little corner store, most restaurants and foodstalls and dispensed by thousands of machines. So is the excellent local beer, "Taiwan" brand.

All sorts of imported alcoholic drinks are available—at a price. The local products, including the beer, come from the Taiwan Tobacco and Wine Monopoly. *Shaohsing*, a strong rice wine usually served warm, is the popular choice at banquets for the many toasts that are drunk. If *Kaoliang* flows instead, watch out! It's as clear and colourless as vodka, but far stronger. There are sure to be frequent calls of *Kanpei!* ("Bottoms up!") in honour of relations and friends, and as a foreign guest, you could be toasted to oblivion.

95

Menu Reader

I'd like . . .	wǒ shyǎng lái yì diǎn	我想來一點 …
apple	píng gwǒ	蘋果
bamboo shoots	jiú sǔn	竹筍
banana	syāng jyaū	香蕉
beef	nyóu ròu	牛肉
beer	pí jyǒu	啤酒
bread	myàn baū	麵包
broccoli	měi gwó huā tsài	美國花菜
chicken	jī ròu	雞肉
clam	hālì	蛤蜊
coffee	kā fēi	咖啡
crab	páng syè	螃蟹
duck	yā ròu	鴨肉
egg	dàn	蛋
fish	yú	魚
fried rice	chǎu-fàn	炒飯
fruit	shwěi gwǒ	水菓
fruit juice	shwěi gwǒ jr̄	水菓汁
mango	máng gwǒ	芒果
milk	nyóu nǎi	牛奶
mineral water	kwàng chuén shwěi	礦泉水
mushrooms	syāng gū	香茹　茹葫
noodles	gān myàn	乾麵
pear	lî	梨
(black) pepper	hú jyaū	糊椒
pineapple	fèng lí	鳳梨
pork	jū ròu	豬肉
prawns	dwèi-syā	對蝦
salt	yán	塩
shrimp	syā(dz)	蝦子
soup	tāng	湯
rice	fàn	飯
sugar	táng	糖
sweet potato	dì gwā	地瓜
spring roll	chūn jǔan	春捲
taro	yú tóu	芋頭
(black) tea	(húng) chá	紅茶
vegetables	shū tsài	蔬菜

BLUEPRINT
FOR A PERFECT TRIP

CONTENTS

AN A–Z SUMMARY
OF PRACTICAL INFORMATION

AIRPORTS. Taipei is served by Chiang Kai-shek (CKS) International Airport, some 40 kilometres (25 mi.) south-west of the capital, a driving time of 40 minutes to well over an hour in heavy traffic. This big modern airport has a currency-exchange counter open 24 hours a day, a restaurant and snack bars, bookstalls, souvenir shops and plenty of free baggage trolleys. The duty-free shop sells tobacco, perfume, wines and spirits to departing and arriving passengers. An information counter helps with inquiries and problems.

There is an international departure tax of NT$300.

Air-conditioned buses run every 15 minutes or so to the main railway station in Taipei and to the Sungshan (domestic) Airport. Some hotels run luxury limousines, some an airport minibus service, and taxis are available. There is a 50 per cent surcharge on the meter fare for taxis doing the airport run.

Sungshan Airport (TSA) is 5 kilometres (3 mi.) north of the centre of Taipei and is used by internal flights. Facilities include shops and snack bars and an information desk.

BICYCLE HIRE. You may be able to hire a bicycle in some of the seaside resorts. Elsewhere, you can arrange a deal with a bicycle shop, but in the big cities air pollution and heavy traffic are somewhat off-putting for cyclists.

CAMPING. Local young people go in for camping trips in the mountains and national parks, and families set up tents at the beach resorts in summer. Equipment can sometimes be hired on site, or from some of the car-rental companies. If you are planning to do much camping, equipment can be bought locally quite economically.

CAR HIRE (see also DRIVING). Major international car-hire firms are not much in evidence in Taiwan, but there are a few local companies, some reliable, others less so. Terms are broadly in line with international rates. It's always advisable to check the tyres and general condition of the car, and full insurance cover is recommended (even though there is a substantial saving if you agree to pay for the first NT$10,000 or so of any damage).

To hire a car, you need an international driving licence and your passport. Most agencies set a minimum age for car hire at 25. Reputable firms accept major credit cards as payment: without one you will be asked for a large cash deposit. The rates on page 112 include tax and fully comprehensive insurance.

Chauffeur-driven cars. This way of sightseeing is more comfortable than driving yourself on busy streets or tortuous mountain roads, but the charge per hour is high. Some garages impose a minimum rental period. Taxis can also be hired by the hour, half-day or day, with prices ranging wildly according to your bargaining skills.

CHILDREN'S TAIWAN. There are many parks and playgrounds for children, as well as a variety of fun parks, such as Dreamland at Wulai. Children will also enjoy the Taipei City Zoo and the Leofoo Safari Park, not to mention the miniatures of China's and the world's great buildings at Window on China. In summer they'll be happy at the northern beaches, while the beaches in the far south can be warm enough even in winter.

Budding scientists will learn a lot at the Science Museum in Taichung: most other museums will appeal mainly to older children—the limited English labelling is a drawback in many cases.

Local families picnic and feed the carp at the Chiang Kai-shek Memorial in Taipei, or fly kites on Sundays at the Sun Yat-sen Memorial. You are welcome to join them. (If you don't have a kite, don't worry; they are on sale there.)

CLIMATE. Taiwan's climate is classified as subtropical, but that can cover a wide variety. Summers, from May to October, are hot and very humid, making the beaches and mountains especially appealing.

During the short winter from December to March it's much cooler but still humid: mists and damp can make it feel chilly. A curious phenomenon, sunshine and fine raindrops at the same time, is so common it has a special name, meaning "sunny rain", in Chinese.

The south and south-west are wetter in summer, mainly dry in winter. The north and east have rainy winters, especially on the north-east coast when it can pour for days on end. Typhoons bring strong winds and heavy rain to Taiwan several times a year between August and October.

The most comfortable months to visit Taiwan are March and April, and from September to November. It's always cooler in the mountains, and January and February bring skiers to one of the highest altitude resorts.

The following chart shows the average daily maximum and minimum temperatures for Taipei.

		J	F	M	A	M	J	J	A	S	O	N	D
Maximum	°F	66	65	70	77	83	89	92	91	88	81	75	69
	°C	19	18	21	25	28	32	33	33	31	27	24	21
Minimum	°F	54	53	57	63	69	73	76	75	73	67	62	57
	°C	12	12	14	17	21	23	24	24	23	19	17	14

Minimum temperatures are measured just before sunrise, maximum temperatures in the afternoon.

CLOTHING. Light and loose cotton clothes (not synthetic fibres) are the best daytime wear for the hot and sticky summer, when you'll also be glad of a hat for protection from the sun. Take comfortable shoes or sandals for sightseeing (some are available locally, though they're unlikely to be high fashion).

Business people can follow local example: men usually wear open-neck shirts, even in offices, in summer. Take a lightweight suit for slightly more formal occasions. Fierce air-conditioning presents a problem. You may be out in heat and humidity resembling a sauna, and then freeze when you come inside.

But the heat doesn't mean you can go around half-dressed. People disapprove of unseemly dress in public places and beachwear away from the beach. Although bikinis are a common sight at beaches, topless sunbathing and nudity are illegal, and you risk a fine or worse if you try.

In the evening, at certain luxury hotels men may be requested to wear a tie; women may need something dressy. Take a sweater or a wrap for cooler winter evenings.

In winter, pack a jacket and sweater. A light raincoat and umbrella may be useful at any time of year: a day that starts with blue skies can often end in rain. Take swimwear even in winter: some hotels have heated indoor pools, and pools fed by hot springs are a therapeutic treat.

COMPLAINTS. If things go wrong, first point out the problem in a pleasant way. If necessary, complain to the owner or manager of the establishment. They will usually try to set things right. If you are still not satisfied, you can try the tourist "hot line" (see p. 116) and only as a last resort go to the police.

If your problem is bad merchandise or car faults, complain at once to the merchant or car-hire firm. If this fails, you could try going to the Tourism Bureau or Taiwan Visitors Association. Complaints made to the police about matters to do with tourism will usually be referred back to these organizations.

CONVERSION CHARTS. Metric weights and measures are in general use, although there are a few survivals from earlier systems, especially in markets.

Fluid measures

Distance

Temperature

Length

Weight

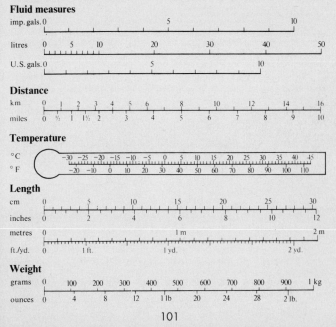

101

CRIME and THEFT. Taiwan is remarkably safe and still mainly free of street crime. But like everywhere else in the world, it's wise to take the usual precautions. Put your valuables in the hotel safe: if you have to carry something of value, don't make it conspicuous. Beware of pickpockets and bag-snatchers, especially in busy markets or on crowded buses or trains. Lock your car as a matter of principle. Any loss or theft should be reported immediately to the nearest police station and, if it occurred at a hotel, to the hotel management.

The possession, use and distribution of drugs are criminal offences, punishable by fines and/or prison.

Police emergency number 110

CUSTOMS and ENTRY REGULATIONS. All visitors need a visa to enter Taiwan, obtainable from one of Taiwan's embassies or consulates. In countries without such representation, a letter of introduction must be obtained from a Taiwan trade or information office. It will then be exchanged for a visa on arrival at an international port of entry to Taiwan. A fee is payable, in New Taiwan Dollars, but this is generally collected on departure, at the same time as the airport departure tax. Visas are normally valid for a stay of up to 60 days. Extensions must be applied for at police headquarters. Certain groups of 15 or more may obtain group visas for a stay of up to two weeks. All members must arrive and leave together.

If arriving from, or having recently passed through, an infected area, you must have current international certificates of vaccination against cholera and yellow fever.

On arrival, you must fill out a customs declaration form (one per family). Here's what you can take into Taiwan duty free and, when returning home, into your own country:

Into:	Cigarettes	Cigars	Tobacco	Spirits	Wine
Taiwan	200 or	25	or 400 g.	1 l. or	1 l.
Canada	200 and	50	and 900 g.	1.1 l. or	1.1 l.
U.K. 1)	200 or	50	or 250 g.	1 l. and	2 l.
U.K. 2)	300 or	75	or 400 g.	1.5 l. and	5 l.
U.S.A.	200 and	100	or 3)	1 l. or	1 l.

1) Duty-free items, which can be combined with: 2) duty-paid items.
3) A reasonable quantity.

No drugs, weapons (even toy copies) or meats (other than canned) may be imported into Taiwan.

Currency restrictions. There's no limit on how much foreign currency a non-resident may bring into Taiwan (large amounts must be declared upon arrival), but you are entitled to import only NT$8,000 in local currency. Visitors may export a maximum of NT$8,000 in local currency, plus any remaining foreign currency of the sum they brought in and declared to customs upon arrival.

Although the NT$ is a solidly backed currency, it's quite difficult to exchange any surplus at a fair rate outside Taiwan. So it makes sense to take as little as possible out of the country if you have no immediate plans to return.

DRIVING IN TAIWAN. To drive your own or another vehicle in Taiwan, you will need an international driving licence, and it is advisable to carry your national driving licence as well.

Seat belts are obligatory on freeways, but it's a safe policy to wear them at all times.

Driving conditions. Driving is on the right. Notice that here you are in a place where rules and regulations are taken as advisory rather than mandatory. Priority seems to go to the driver with the confidence to take it. The best policy for visitors is to drive defensively, giving a wide berth to lorries (trucks), aggressive buses and pushy taxis.

Speed limits are clearly marked, 40, 50 or 60 kph in built-up areas, 70 or 80 kph on main roads and 90 kph on "freeways".

In Taipei, one-way streets, restricted turns and lack of direction signs in anything other than Chinese characters can be a trial for the newcomer. Everywhere, squadrons of motor scooters buzz like bees, filtering to the front at red lights and then turning across the rest of the traffic as it starts to move.

Road conditions. Some roads are smooth and broad, but many more are potholed and narrow. There is commonly a deep gully along one side: put a wheel in there and your car will suffer major damage. In the mountains, there may be a precipice on the other side.

Country and mountain roads are subject to landslips and rockfalls caused by rain and earth tremors: the job of the road engineers is never finished.

High passes and remote roads may be narrow and unpaved. "Never on Sunday" is a good rule for these, for on that one day of the week they can be crowded with cars and unofficial taxis, engagingly known as "wild chickens".

Be careful if you go exploring by car—you may get on a road or country path that narrows down so much that you have to back out. It's best to use the horn when going round sharp corners and hairpin turns, especially in villages.

On "freeways"—actually toll roads—you'll be overtaken (passed) on both sides simultaneously, with some speedsters using the hard shoulder. At the toll booths, don't take the left-hand lanes unless you have the exact amount of money, or you will lose whatever change was due. And don't take the far right lanes, unless you want to pay the higher rate for buses and trucks.

Parking. Fines for illegal parking are sometimes enforced. Be absolutely sure not to block anyone, or an exit, or overstay on parking meters. The authorities may decide to crack down on offenders and bring in the tow trucks. Wrongly parked scooters are "arrested" by the dozen and carted off.

If you put your car in a parking lot, give the attendant a small tip when you leave.

Fuel and oil. Plenty of stations are scattered around the main towns and cities, with advance warning signs (giving the distance and opening hours). There are fewer stations in remote areas so don't set off into the mountains with a near-empty tank. Diesel fuel is widely available: a few stations carry lead-free.

Breakdowns. Towing and on-the-spot repairs are made by local garages, and spare parts can usually be found for most common makes of car. Taiwan's mechanics are skilled, but you should get a detailed estimate before you let them start work. If you're renting your car, first call the hire firm who should be able to send help within the hour.

Accidents. In case of an accident, call the police immediately (dial 110). It is wise not to move your vehicle until they arrive, since accident claims are more easily settled if the police make a report on the spot.

ELECTRIC CURRENT. Electric supply is 110 volt, 60 cycle A.C. like the U.S. system. British, Australian and New Zealand visitors will need an adaptor.

EMBASSIES and CONSULATES. These and other representatives of foreign countries in Taiwan are all in Taipei:

Australia   The Australian Commerce and Industry Office, 26F, Room 2605, 333 Keelung Road Section 1, Taipei; tel. (02) 720 2833

Canada   Canadian Trade Office in Taipei, 13F, 365 Fuhsing North Road, Taipei; tel. (02) 713 7268

New Zealand   New Zealand Commerce and Industry Office, Room 0812, 8th Floor, 333 Keelung Road Section 1, Taipei; tel. (02) 757 7060

South Africa   Embassy of the Republic of South Africa, 13F, Bank Tower, 205 Tunhua North Road, Taipei; tel. (02) 715 3250

United Kingdom   Anglo-Taiwan Trade Committee, 9th Floor, 99 Jenai Road Section 2, Taipei; tel. (02) 322 4242

U.S.A.   American Institute in Taiwan, 7, Lane 134, Hsinyi Road Section 3, Taipei; tel. (02) 709 2000

EMERGENCIES. In case of accident or other emergencies, phone:

Police   110
Ambulance   119
Fire   119

ETIQUETTE (see also MEETING AND GREETING). The Chinese have evolved quite strict codes of conduct to regulate relations between themselves. They are, however, forgiving of unconscious transgressions by foreigners, which they've learned to expect. But try to follow local custom wherever you can. Being courteous and polite is the first requirement of good behaviour. The second is the rule of reciprocity, which applies at every level. Favours large and small are expected to be returned in due course; if someone pays you compliments, find a way to return them; if they give a banquet for you, praise the food—and remember, it will be your turn to be host later, perhaps when they visit your country. (Business entertaining very rarely happens in homes, but almost always over a meal—often an elaborate one—in a restaurant.)

Turn up punctually for appointments: time is money and days are busy in Taiwan. The people you meet on business are all attention—until the allotted span of the meeting nears its end. Then you'll find an efficient farewell routine going into action and you'll be out in the street before you know it, exactly on the hour or half-hour.

If you expect to be visiting Chinese people in their homes, you'll need to take some small gifts, so it's a good idea to bring something suitable from your home country. Don't expect your gift to be opened right away: it will be set aside with appropriate murmurings for later.

Try never to shout or lose your temper. Always stay calm and cool. Be modest and respectful, the more so with anyone older or more senior. And if all this sounds rather serious, it isn't. People here smile and laugh a lot, and mean it.

GETTING TO TAIWAN. Considering the wide variety of fares and regulations and the choice of ways to go, you'll be well advised to consult a reliable travel agent. That way you have the best chance of meeting your timetable and budget.

By air. Taipei's Chiang Kai-shek Airport (see p. 98) is linked by non-stop international flights to many cities in the Far East (most frequently to Hong Kong, Singapore and Tokyo), and to Los Angeles and San Francisco. In addition, there are direct flights from Amsterdam and Vienna, Johannesburg and certain Middle Eastern cities. Travellers from other points will normally have to fly to one of these for connecting flights to Taiwan.

Kaohsiung airport in south-western Taiwan has international flights to Hong Kong, Tokyo, Osaka and Bangkok.

Ask about lower fares for children, youths, students and senior citizens, excursions and night flights as well as inclusive holidays.

By sea. There is an international ferry service once a week from Kaohsiung and Keelung in Taiwan to and from Okinawa, Japan, and on to the other main Japanese islands. Another line sails weekly from Kaohsiung to and from Macao on the south China coast. Ask your travel agent for the departure dates and prices.

GUIDES. The Tourist Guide Association, on the 9th floor of the same building as the Taiwan Visitors Association (see TOURIST INFORMATION OFFICES), can provide you with qualified official guides (tel. 02-592 2207). Major hotels can also find a guide for you. Tipping is optional.

HAIRDRESSERS. Taiwan's better hairdressers are generally well up on the latest styles and cuts. Services can include a skilled head-massage and manicure. Some barber's shops offer other sorts of massage. In certain cases this is a cover for less legitimate activities. Many of the bigger hotels have good hairdressing salons.

HEALTH and MEDICAL CARE. In the heat of summer, as in many similar climates, newcomers may contract "tourist's tummy", often due to fatigue, too much sun and change of diet. Food and drink in hotels and restaurants are generally safe. Food from street stalls may well be excellent, but it is safer to eat only from places that are clearly hygienic; stick to cooked items. If at all possible, make sure all fruit and salads are washed first, in clean water. If gastro-intestinal or other problems last more than a day or two, see a doctor.

Beware of the sun, which is powerful in the summer months and at high altitude any time of year. Start with a sunscreen or total-block cream at first and build up a tan gradually in small doses. The occasional salt tablet doesn't do any harm when you're sweating a lot.

Malaria has been eradicated, but mosquitoes can still be annoying. If they're a problem, in country areas and non-air-conditioned rooms, buy an inexpensive coil which smoulders all night and keeps them away. Even more effective (and more expensive) is the electric version. Both can be purchased at chemists.

Medical insurance. Make sure your travel insurance policy covers accident or illness while on holiday—it's simply a wise precaution.

Treatment. Medical treatment is usually of a high standard. General practitioners are well qualified and equipment is good.

If you need a doctor urgently, your hotel will help you find one; otherwise, the chemist/pharmacist can be of assistance. In an emergency, you can dial 119.

Traditional Chinese therapies and remedies are still practised and highly regarded, and the relatively low cost of such treatments attracts people from other countries in the region. There are many skilled acupuncturists, for example, working in Taiwan. (Others may be less well qualified. For this reason, and because scrupulous hygiene is essential in the use of needles, only practitioners with the highest recommendation should be consulted.)

Massage. Many hotel fitness centres and hot-spring resorts can offer an appointment with a masseur, or more often, a blind masseuse, for in

China massage is a vocation traditionally taken up by blind people. As in some countries in the region, it can be a cover for less legitimate activities.

Pharmacies. Some chain stores have a pharmacy department, and there are many independent pharmacies as well, all of them open during normal working and shopping hours. A few are marked with a red cross. Taiwan is a major producer of drugs that are normally sold on prescription in other countries.

Vaccinations. Cholera, typhoid and polio vaccinations are recommended.

HITCH-HIKING. It is legal and fairly easy in country areas: in the cities, you're more likely to attract a taxi than a free ride. If you try hitching, take the normal precautions. But it makes sense to use the cheap and perfectly adequate bus services.

HOURS. Hours of opening vary widely according to the establishment, whether government or private, the day of the week, the time of year. The following is an indication of the general rules. (See also under COMMUNICATIONS and MONEY MATTERS.)

Government offices. 8.30 a.m. to 12.30 p.m., and 1.30 to 5.30 p.m., Monday to Friday, and 8.30 a.m. to 12.30 p.m. Saturday.

Offices and Businesses. 8.30 or 9 a.m. to 5 or 5.30 p.m., Monday to Friday. Some operate on Saturday mornings, 8.30 or 9 a.m. to noon. Most head or managing offices follow government schedules.

Shops. Many are open from 9 a.m. to 9 p.m. daily. Department stores usually open about 10 a.m. and close at about 9.30 p.m. Some smaller establishments may close for an hour or so during lunch. "Night markets" run from sunset to midnight or even later.

Museums. Most museums and sites are state run and have fairly uniform hours, opening daily from 9 a.m. to 5 p.m. If there is a closing day, it is generally Monday.

Temples are typically open for worship from 7 a.m. to about 10 p.m. Visitors are welcome as long as they don't intrude on ceremonies or otherwise cause a disturbance.

Restaurants. Lunch runs roughly from noon to 2 p.m., dinner from 6 p.m. to 9 or 9.30 p.m. in the big cities, but perhaps only to 7.30 p.m. in country areas and mountain resorts—even in the hotels there. Night market eating places flourish from about 7 to 11 p.m.

LANGUAGE. The official language is Mandarin Chinese. Especially in country areas and in the south, many people speak the Taiwanese dialect. Standard Chinese script is used—it makes sense to users of all the main dialects. English is the most widely taught foreign language, and is understood by many professional and business people, but by few people in the street.

The usual form in which Chinese words (especially proper names) are rendered into Roman script is based on the Wade-Giles system, and not the Pinyin adopted by mainland China and many Western scholars (recognizable by its use of q and x). Unfortunately, in Taiwan Wade-Giles tends to be applied inconsistently.

There is no consensus about running syllables into one word or hyphenating, or whether to capitalize the second part. For example: Chung Shan, Chung-Shan, Chung-shan and Chungshan (and the Mandarin name of Sun Yat-sen) are all in use for the name of a main road in Taipei. This book uses the single word form except where another usage is practically universal (as indeed with Sun Yat-sen, Chiang Kai-shek, and most people's given name in Taiwan).

LAUNDRY and DRY-CLEANING. There are plenty of rapid laundry and dry-cleaning services, and hotels offer same-day service. The high humidity means that you'll get through a lot of clothes: it's convenient to carry some detergent and plastic hangers and do some of your own washing.

LOST PROPERTY. Check first where you think you lost the object. If you can't find it there, report the loss at the nearest police station, if only to obtain a paper to accompany any insurance claim.

MAIL

Post offices. 8 a.m.–6 p.m., Monday to Saturday, 8 a.m. to noon on Sundays.

Poste restante (general delivery). If you wish to have your mail sent to you c/o poste restante, you should write ahead of time to warn the post office (address the letter to the Postmaster General, General Post Office, Taipei, Taiwan).

Telegrams can be sent from main post offices, but remember that there is little point in sending telegrams to the U.K., where they are only delivered with the mail. Better to use the direct-dial telephone.

Telex. Your hotel may have a telex that you can use. Public telex facilities are available at main offices of the I.T.A. (the telecommunications administration).

Fax. For companies and for many individuals, fax is a way of life in Taiwan. Facsimile transmission services are available at most larger hotels and at main offices of the I.T.A.

MAPS. It is hard to find detailed and accurate maps of Taiwan, though the Tourism Bureau publishes good city street plans and a simple map of the whole island. It is useful to have the names of places in both Chinese and Roman script so that you can ask local people the way by pointing at the map.

If you're driving, you need a map with road numbers: they are one of the few clues you'll get in some areas where direction signs are only in Chinese characters.

The maps in this book have been prepared by Falk-Verlag, Hamburg.

MEETING and GREETING. The traditional deep bow of earlier times has given way to a firm handshake, with an accompanying smile and a slight nod of the head (especially to someone older or senior, and at first-time meetings). The same smile and nod—without the handshake—is a common way of politely acknowledging strangers in, say, a hotel corridor. More physical greetings—backslaps, hugs and shoulder squeezes—are not appreciated.

Name cards are exchanged at all but the most transitory of encounters. If you don't have cards with you at all times, you scarcely exist. Mumbled excuses about having "run out of cards" won't save you from a catastrophic loss of face. So don't arrive in Taiwan without a large supply, or, if you do, have some printed right away, but take extreme precautions against misprints. If you can find an expert to devise a Chinese version of your name, have that printed on the reverse of your cards.

It's good manners to present any piece of paper, your card included, with both hands. You'll have to devise your own way of doing this while accepting a card at the same time. Politeness demands that you read a card carefully when it is presented to you.

Names. In Chinese names, the surname (family name) usually comes first. So you would address a man called Chung Chi-kuo as "Mr Chung". But watch out for names whose owners have reversed them when putting them into Latin script.

Many people have taken a Western-type "first name" as well, or been given one by their English teachers. So the above person might call himself, for example, James Chung Chi-kuo.

MONEY MATTERS

Currency. The New Taiwan Dollar (NT$) is divided into 100 cents (c).
   Notes: NT$ 50, 100, 500, 1,000
   Coins: NT$ 1, 5, 10
   For currency restrictions, see under CUSTOMS AND ENTRY REGULATIONS.

Banking hours. 9 a.m. to 3.30 p.m., Monday to Friday, 9 a.m. to noon on Saturdays. Many hotels give low rates of exchange for foreign cash and traveller's cheques, so it's usually better to go to one of the banks permitted to deal in foreign exchange. You'll need your passport when cashing traveller's cheques.

Credit cards are widely accepted by better shops, hotels and restaurants, but in the bigger cities only. Usually the symbols of the cards accepted are on display. You can often negotiate a discount for cash, however. That includes many hotel prices, particularly at resorts on weekdays when business is slow.

Prices are usually fixed in the bigger shops, but you can try your bargaining skills at market stalls, street stands and some smaller places. Some prices are listed on page 112 as a guideline.

MOUNTAIN PERMITS.
Certain areas where the aboriginal tribes live may only be entered if you have a special pass. For some places this is issued at an entrance gate or local police post, or in Taipei at the Foreign Affairs Office, Taiwan Provincial Police Administration, 7 Chunghsiao E. Road Section 1, Taipei. You will need two passport-size photos.

NEWSPAPERS and MAGAZINES.
The *Asian Wall Street Journal* and the *International Herald Tribune* are usually available in the afternoon of the day of publication at news-stands in Taipei and Kaohsiung. The Hong Kong English-language papers are also available in main cities. The *China Post* and *China News* are English-language daily newspapers published in Taipei, with local, mainland and international news. Many American, European and Hong Kong magazines are on sale. *This Month in Taiwan* and *Taipei* magazines are useful for finding out about forthcoming events and entertainment.

PHOTOGRAPHY. Taipei has several good photography shops and some of the best-known film brands are available. You may have trouble buying 35-mm black-and-white or especially fast film, but colour print film is sold almost everywhere. Transparency (slide) film is hard to find outside the big cities.

Fast black-and-white development is rare. Colour print film is processed the same day on weekdays.

The airport X-ray machines do not spoil normal film, but for safety's sake, you can put it in a bag to be checked separately.

Video tape is readily available, in full or camcorder size.

PLANNING YOUR BUDGET

To give you an idea of what to expect, here's a list of average prices in New Taiwan Dollars (NT$ or TWD). They can only be approximate, especially where competing prices prevail (e.g., car hire, souvenirs).

Airport transfer. CKS to city centre: taxi NT$1,000, bus NT$75, hotel bus NT$350, hotel special limousine NT$1,500.

Baby-sitters. NT$200 per hour.

Car hire. NT$1,200 per day and up (unlimited mileage).

Cigarettes. Local brands NT$25, imported NT$45.

Food and drinks. Typical meal in medium-priced local restaurant NT$150–400, bottle of wine NT$500, soft drink NT$30, coffee NT$30, beer NT$50.

Guided tours. NT$500 per half-day city tour; NT$1,000 and up for out-of-town day-trips; NT$2,500 per day, including accommodation but not meals, for longer tours of the island.

Hairdressers. *Woman's* haircut, shampoo and blow-dry NT$300 and up. *Man's* haircut and blow-dry NT$150 and up.

Hotels. Per person sharing twin room, per night, with breakfast. De luxe hotel NT$3,000; mid-range NT$1,800; budget NT$900.

Shopping bag. Loaf of bread NT$40 for 500 grams, butter NT$25 per 250 grams, milk NT$35 per bottle, instant coffee NT$90 per 100 grams, wine NT$250 per bottle, whisky/gin NT$650 per bottle, soft drinks NT$15, beer NT$30 per can.

Souvenirs. Postcards NT$5–10; wood-carving NT$500 and up; kite NT$100 and up; paper lantern NT$300 and up.

Sports. Golf, green fee NT$1,500; river-rafting NT$700 for 4-hour trip; windsurfer rental NT$400 per hour.

Transport. *Taxi* NT$35–40 for the first 1.5 km., NT$5 for each extra 350 metres. *Buses* NT$10 per city ride. *Intercity buses:* Taipei–Tainan NT$350. *Trains:* Taipei–Hualien NT$300. *Internal flights:* Taipei–Kaohsiung NT$1,100.

POLICE. Most towns have a police station, clearly marked. Some stations are not manned around the clock. Don't hesitate to approach police officers: they are friendly although their English is likely to be limited or non-existent.

Try to contact the police immediately in case of a car accident (see under DRIVING). In an emergency, call the police on 110. Again, you'll probably need a translator.

PUBLIC HOLIDAYS. These are the official civic and religious holidays, when banks, offices and most shops are closed.

January 1 and 2	Foundation Day/ New Year's Day
March 29	Youth Day
April 5 (April 4 in leap years)	Tomb Sweeping Day
May 1	Labour Day
September 28	Confucius Day/ Teachers' Day
October 10	National Day ("Double Ten" Day)
October 25	Restoration Day
October 31	Chiang Kai-shek's Birthday
November 12	Dr. Sun Yat-sen's Birthday
December 25	Constitution Day

Moveable dates: Chinese Lunar New Year (generally 3–5 days—depending on where the weekend falls—in late-January to mid-February); Dragon Boat Festival (generally a day in late May or early June); Mid-Autumn Festival (generally late September or early October).

Many other days are designated as festivals or commemorations, but are not public holidays.

113

RADIO and TV. There is a local AM/FM radio channel mostly in English, with rock/pop music and news on the hour. Some English-language programmes appear on the three channels of local TV. Check the English-language press for details. Some hotels relay CNN, Japanese and other satellite channels.

On short-wave bands, reception of the BBC World Service is clear. Voice of America programmes can also be picked up easily.

RELIGIOUS SERVICES. As well as countless Buddhist and Taoist temples and shrines, Taiwan has churches of several Christian sects, and mosques, synagogues and Bahai centres. Many are listed in *This Month in Taiwan*, with addresses and telephone numbers. Taipei's various Sunday Christian services are listed in Saturday's *China Post*.

SMOKING. Cigarettes and tobacco are available in many small shops and market stalls. Some international brands are sold, and cigarettes are also made locally by the tobacco monopoly. Local makes are less expensive than foreign ones. Major international brands of cigars and tobacco are also on sale.

TELEPHONE. The main office of the telecommunications administration (I.T.A.), is at 28 Hangchou South Road Section 1, Taipei; tel. (02) 344 3781 (open 24 hours).

Public telephone boxes take NT$1, 5 and 10 coins. The charge for local calls is very low—NT$1 for three minutes. Unfortunately, in the older boxes, the line is then broken, and you have to start again. There are growing numbers of card-phone boxes which is much more convenient.

Overseas calls can be dialled direct to many countries, from major hotels or certain international call boxes, using the code 002 followed by the destination code. Hotels will usually add an extra charge for calls placed.

For the international directory of enquiries and information service, and for the overseas exchange, dial 100.

International direct dialling enquiries (02) 321 2535.

English-language assistance service (02) 311 6796.

The country code for Taiwan when dialling from elsewhere is 886.

TIME DIFFERENCES. Taiwan time is GMT + 8, with no seasonal adjustments. The following chart indicates standard time differences.

New York 7 a.m.	London noon	**Taipei** **8 p.m.**	Sydney 9 p.m.

TIPPING. A 10 per cent service charge (plus 5% V.A.T.) is included in hotel and restaurant bills, and tips on top of this are not expected, unless some exceptional extra service has been given. A bit of loose change for their services is appreciated by bellboys, hat-check attendants, etc. The chart below gives some suggestions as to how much to leave.

Porter, per bag	NT$20 per bag
Taxi driver	round fare upwards by small amount (if change is due, drivers will routinely keep NT$5 or 10 as a tip)
Hairdresser/Barber	10–15%

TOILETS. There are few public conveniences and only in the larger towns, and the signs designating "ladies" or "gentlemen" may be in Chinese characters. But they abound at tourist sites, and petrol (gas) stations, hotels, restaurants, cafés and bars usually have facilities you can use. In rural areas they may be the "hole in the floor" variety. Paper is often absent: it's advisable to carry a pack of tissues yourself.

TOURIST INFORMATION OFFICES. At the Tourist Information Service Centre at Chiang Kai-shek International Airport, Taipei, receptionists will help with transport and accommodation too.

The Travel Information Service Centre at Sungshan (Domestic) Airport, Taipei, is mainly for local people going abroad, but it does feature the attractions of Taiwan as well.

The office to contact for detailed brochures, maps and much other information on Taiwan is the Tourism Bureau at:

9 F, 290 Chunghsiao East Road, Section 4, (PO Box 1490), Taipei; tel. (02) 721 8541

The Taiwan Visitors Association also publishes useful books and leaflets. It has its main office at:

5 F, 111 Minchuan East Road, Taipei; tel. (02) 594 3261

In case of problems or questions, you can call the special "hot line" number, (02) 717 3737. This number is staffed by English-speakers every day from 8 a.m. to 8 p.m., but at all other times a recording machine registers calls.

Information on Taiwan abroad:

Australia: Far East Trading Co. Pty. Ltd., Suite 2409, Level 24, MLC Centre, Martin Place, Sydney NSW 2000; tel. (2) 231 6942; fax (2) 233 7752.

Canada: via New York office.

Republic of Ireland: via London office.

New Zealand: East Asia Trade Centre, 7/F I.B.M. House (P.O. Box 10-250), 155-161 The Terrace, Wellington; tel. 736 474

South Africa: 1147 Schoeman Street, Hatfield, Pretoria 0083; tel. (012) 436071/3

United Kingdom: Free Chinese Centre, 4th Floor, Dorland House, 14–16 Regent Street; London SW1Y 4PH; tel. (071) 930 5767

U.S.A.: CCNAA, 4201 Wisconsin Avenue NW, Washington DC 20016; tel. (202) 895 1819
Tourism Representative, Travel Section, CCNAA Office, Suite 8855, 1 World Trade Center, New York, NY 10048; tel. (212) 466 0691/2

TRANSPORT

Bus services. Within Taipei you have a choice of regular or (slightly more expensive) air-conditioned buses. Sometimes you pay when boarding, other times when getting off. Follow the example of your fellow passengers. You can buy books of tickets from kiosks, often situated near bus stops. There is an experiment under way with automatic ticket machines. Plans are to introduce these on all city buses in the future.

Inter-city express services too may be regular or air-conditioned. The latter's dark windows rather obscure the view and spoil any photographs taken through them. Travel sickness bags are provided, and you may find you'll need them on the twisting mountain roads.

There may be more than one main terminal per city, operated by different companies serving different destinations. At these main terminals, tickets are sold in advance, and not normally more than there are seats on the bus. Numbered seats are rare, so there can be a rush for the best when the bus arrives. At other stops, in rural areas, the usual politeness and discipline may break down entirely in the boarding process.

Ferries. One of the more enjoyable ways of travelling, if you have a little time to spare, is to take a ferry to one of the offshore islands.

Kaohsiung is the point of departure for ferries to Penghu (the Pescadores).

Domestic flights. With an "open skies" policy of competition, a number of different airlines operate regular flights between the main cities, with many flights a day between Taipei (Sungshan Airport) and Kaohsiung, and others serving Hualien, Taitung, Taichung. Green Island, Lanyu (Orchid Island), Makung on Penghu and Kinmen are among the smaller islands linked to one or more of these cities daily. In bad weather, be prepared for disruptions to the schedules, especially on the inter-island routes.

Taxis. Within the cities you should have no problem finding a taxi: it is more likely that one will find you, even if you don't need it. The drivers like to keep up a high speed, regardless of road conditions: even the government's Tourism Bureau says Taipei's taxis will provide a "thrilling, memorable experience".

It's a good idea to carry a card from your hotel—or the address of wherever else you want to go—in Chinese characters, to show the driver who is unlikely to speak much or any English (and your pronunciation of Chinese names may only confuse the issue).

Taxi drivers should always switch on their meters: ask them to do so by simply pointing at the meter if they don't. They are permitted to make a surcharge of 50 per cent between CKS International Airport and Taipei, and a surcharge for trips during rush hour and late at night—between 11 p.m. and 5 a.m.

Taxis in smaller towns and in the countryside have no meters. Try to determine what the fare will be before getting in. (About NT$50 is normal within an average town). This is even more important if you have to take one of the unlicensed "wild chicken" taxis that go looking for business when the police aren't watching. In country areas they're instantly recognizable: big, black, battered cars which gather at important road junctions.

Trains. Taiwan's trains are frequent, comfortable, efficient and inexpensive. Lines run down both the west and the spectacular east coast and link all the main cities. You must reserve seats on the express and air-conditioned trains (there are three classes with slightly differing prices, depending on comfort and speed). You can make reservations up to three days ahead. Return (round-trip) tickets carry a discount, but you cannot reserve the return journey seat at the original point of departure.

Taipei's fine main station has a tourist information office and a detailed, bilingual display showing arrivals and departures and the class of train.

Note: you should carry your passport when travelling, even within Taiwan. It's needed if you want to get permits to enter certain mountain areas, and also to board domestic flights and for ferry trips to some islands. Hotel registration clerks usually ask for it too. It is also a good idea to carry some spare passport photos on you for various purposes, including for obtaining mountain permits (see p. 111).

YOUTH and RECREATION HOSTELS. In the big cities and in the mountains—especially the national parks—various organizations run hostels large and small. They're intended mainly for youth groups and offer dormitory accommodation, single-sex, for a minimal fee, and foreign visitors are welcome to stay when they have space. On weekdays, out of the cities, you may have a whole dorm to yourself. There's no particular age limit, and if you don't want to share a dormitory and communal washing facilities, there may also be conventional rooms with rates at the lower end of the hotel price range.

In rural areas and on some of the smaller islands, hotels themselves may have dormitories as well as normal rooms. If you are on a tight budget, ask.

WATER. Drinking water served in hotels and restaurants should have been purified, boiled or distilled. Some hotels have a separate drinking water outlet in their bathrooms. Water from regular taps (faucets) in hotels and homes may not be safe for drinking. Nor may water from fountains. It is a good precaution to carry purifying tablets and a container to keep a supply of drinking water. Local and some imported mineral waters are available.

Soft drinks exist in vast profusion, with vending machines widely distributed.

USEFUL EXPRESSIONS

Hello (How are you?)	nǐ hǎu	你好
Good morning	dzǎu; dzǎu ān	早；早安
Good bye	dzài jyàn	再見
Please	chǐng	請
Thank you	syè sye	謝謝
You're welcome	bú syè	不謝
Yes/No	shì de/bú shì	是的 / 不是
Excuse me (I'm sorry).	dwèi bu chǐ	對不起
Help me, please.	chǐng bāng wǒ máng	請幫我忙。
I'm lost.	wǒ mí lù le	我迷路了。
I don't understand.	wǒ bù dǒng	我不懂。
good/bad	hǎu/hwài	好 / 壞
big/small	dà/syǎu	大 / 小
cheap/expensive	pyányi/gwèi	便宜 / 昂貴
near/far	jìn/ywǎn	近 / 遠
old/new	jyòu/syīn	舊 / 新
old/young	nyán lǎu/nyán chīng	年老 / 年青
beautiful/ugly	měi (lì)/nán kàn	美麗 / 丑陋
How much?	dwō shǎu	多少錢
Is this drinking water?	jèi shì yǐn yòng shwěi ma	這是飲用水嗎？
Where are the toilets?	tse swǒ dzài náli	廁所在哪裡？
I need a doctor.	wǒ yàu jyàu yí wèi yī shēng	我要叫一位醫生
I'd like a taxi.	wǒ syū yāu jyàu yí lyàng chū dzū chì chē	我需要叫一輛出租汽車。
Go straight.	yì jŕ dzǒu	一直走
Turn left/Turn right.	dzwǒ jwàn/yò jwàn	左轉 / 右轉
Slow down/ Go faster.	màn yì dyǎn/ kwài yì dyǎn	慢一轉 / 快一點
Please wait a minute.	chǐng děng yí sỳa	請等一下
Please stop here.	chǐng tíng chē	請停車
Hotel	lyú gwǎn	旅館
Museum/ Gallery	bwó wù gwǎn/ hwà láng	博物館 / 畫廊
Park	gūng ywǎn	公園
Hospital	yī ywàn	醫院
Train station	hwǒ chē jàn	火車站
Bus station	gūng chē jàn	公車站
Restaurant	fàn gwǎn	飯館

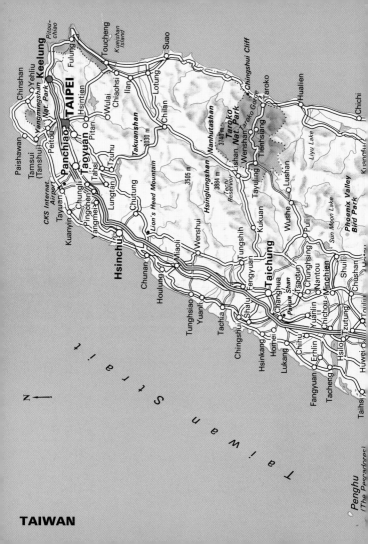

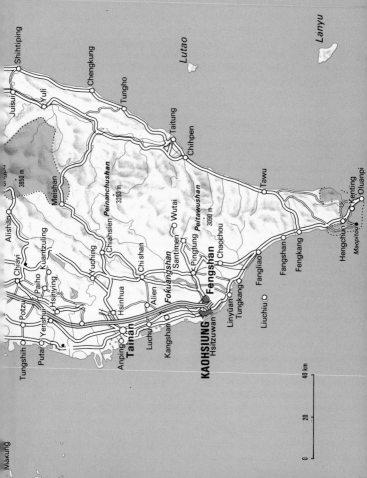

Makung

Tungshih

Putai

Chiayi

Potzu

Yenshui Hsinying

Kuantzuling

Paiho

Alishan

3950 m

Meishan

Juisui

Yuli

Shihtiping

Chengkung

Tungho

Lutao

Lanyu

Yuching

Chiahsien Peinanchushan

3293 m

Taitung

Chihpen

Luchu

Tainan

Anping

Hsitzuwan

KAOHSIUNG

Fengshan

Fokuangshan

Chi-shan

Pingtung Peitawushan

Santimen

3090 m

Wutai

Chaochou

Tawu

Kenting

Oluanpi

Hengchun

Maopitou

Fengkang

Fangshan

Fangliao

Liuchiu

Tungkang

Linyüan

Kangshan

Hsinhua

Alien

0   20   40 km

PLACE NAMES

TAIWAN

Alishan	阿里山
Anping	安平
Aoti	澳堤
Changhua	彰化
Chiaohsi	礁溪
Chiayi	嘉義
Chichi	磯碕海水浴場
Chihnan Temple	指南宮
Chihpen	知本
Chingshui Cliff	清水斷崖
Chinshan	金山
Chunghsing	中興新村
Chungli	中壢
CKS International Airport	中正國際機場
Coral Lake	珊瑚潭
Fangliao	枋寮
Fengyuan	豐原
Fokuangshan	佛光山
Fukueichiao	福奎橋
Fulung	福隆
Green Bay	格林灣
Green Island (Lutao)	綠島
Hsinchu	新竹
Hsitou	溪頭
Hualien	花蓮
Ilan	宜蘭
Juisui	瑞穗
Kaohsiung	高雄市
Keelung	基隆
Kenting National Park	墾丁國家公園
Kuantzuling	關子嶺
Kueishan Island	奎山島
Kukuan	谷關
Lailai	萊萊
Lanyu (Orchid Island)	蘭嶼
Leofoo Safari Park	六福村野生動物園
Lion's Head Mountain	獅頭山
Lishan	梨山
Liuchiu	柳丘
Liyu Lake	鯉魚潭
Lukang	鹿港
Lungtan	龍潭
Lungtung	龍東
Lushan	盧山
Makung	馬公
Maopitou	貓鼻頭
Nanya	南亞
Oluanpi	鵝鑾鼻
Paishawan	白沙灣
Pakua Shan	八卦山
Peikang Temple	北港
Peimen Temple	裴門寺
Peitou	北投
Penghu (The Pescadores)	澎湖群島
Pingtung	屏東
Pitan	碧潭
Pitouchiao	鼻頭角
Sanchung	山村
Sanhsia	山下
Santiaochiao	三條橋
Santimen	三地門
Shanlinhsi	杉林溪
Shihfen Waterfall	西汾瀑布

Shihlin	西嶺	Yehliu	野柳
Shihmen Dam	石門水庫	Yenliao	塩寮
Shihtiping	石梯坪	Yushan (Mt. Jade)	玉山
Suao	蘇澳	Yushan National	玉山國
Sun Moon Lake	日月潭	Park	家公園
Tahsi	大溪		
Taichung	台中		
Tainan	台南		
Taipei	台北市	**TAIPEI**	
Taitung	台東		
Tali	臺里	Chiang Kai-shek	
Tanshui	淡水	Memorial Hall	中正紀念堂
Taoyuan	桃園	Confucian Temple	孔子廟
Taroko	太魯閣	Grand Hotel	圓山大飯店
Taroko Gorge	太魯閣峽谷	Hsingtien Temple	行天宮
Taroko National		Lungshan Temple	龍山寺
Park	太魯閣國家公園	Main railway station	台北火車站
Tawu	大武	Martyrs' Shrine	忠烈祠
Techi Dam	德基水庫	National Museum	歷史博物舘
Tienhsiang	天祥	of History	藝術舘
Tienmu	天母	National Palace	國立故宮
Toucheng	頭城	Museum	博物院
Tsaoling	草嶺	National Theatre	國立劇院
Tsaotun	草屯	and Concert Hall	與音樂廳
Tsengwen Dam	曾文水庫	Presidential Building	總統府
Tungpu	東埔	Sun Yat-sen	
Tungshih	東勢	Memorial Hall	國父紀念舘
Tzuhu	慈湖	Sungshan Airport	松山機場
Wenshan	文山	Taipei Fine Arts	台北市立
Window on China	小人國	Museum	美術舘
Wufeng Temple	吳鳳廟	Taipei International	台北國際會議
Wufengchi Waterfall	五峯旗瀑布	Convention Center	中心
Wulai	烏來	Taipei World Trade	台北世界貿易
Wushe	霧社	Center	中心
Yangmingshan		Taiwan Provincial	
National Park	陽明山國家公園	Museum	博物舘

123

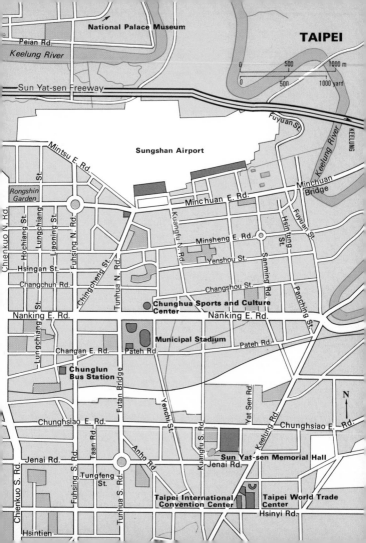